The Scottish Football Book No 25

THE SCOTTISH FOOTBALL BOOK NO 25

Edited by Hugh Taylor

Stanley Paul, London

Stanley Paul & Co. Ltd
3 Fitzroy Square, London W1P 6JD

An imprint of the Hutchinson Publishing Group

London Melbourne Sydney Auckland
Wellington Johannesburg and agencies
throughout the world

First published 1979
© Stanley Paul & Co. Ltd 1979

Typeset at Input Typesetting Ltd

Printed in Great Britain by The Anchor Press Ltd
and bound by Wm Brendon & Son Ltd
both of Tiptree, Essex

ISBN 0 09 139281 0

Black and white photographs by courtesy of *The Evening Times* and
Sportapics.
Colour photographs of the Internationals, Colin Jackson and Alex
MacDonald in the Scottish Cup Final, Rangers v Celtic, Aberdeen v
Dundee Utd, Alan Hansen by Colorsport; all others by Sportapics

Frontispiece:

**What a leap! Doug Somner of Partick Thistle
rises above them all in this match against
Hibernian**

CONTENTS

THE EDITOR SAYS...

To all readers, old and new, a warm welcome to *The Scottish Football Book*, celebrating its quarter century.

How, as they say, time does fly. But things don't change all that much in football, do they?

Once again there are moans about the display of the Scotland team, given a lesson by world champions Argentina. But when weren't we moaning about our teams? Anyhow, the lads keep coming back and there are signs that, under manager Jock Stein, the right blend is being found. But, remember, it takes a long, long time to find the right formula – and the right players to make it work.

On the brighter side, the race for the Premier League last season, won by Celtic, was the most dramatic in history and it looks as though it will be even more competitive this term, with Rangers desperate to pip Celtic and other clubs making a charge.

It was, however, a winter of discontent, with the severe weather disrupting the programme.

Soccer, nevertheless, remains a winter game but it would be sensible if our officials realized an ice age seems to be approaching and did more than hibernate when Siberian weather hits us. There must be a great deal they can do to make sure that our national sport copes better in future in the cold spells we have come to expect.

Surely in this highly technological age science and soccer should get it together to find an acceptable answer.

Rangers didn't win the treble but they put up fine displays in Europe, which boosted our national prestige; Celtic showed valour far above the call of duty; Dundee United kept up a spirited challenge and so there was little wrong with the Premier League. It was good to see Dundee and Kilmarnock returning to the highest division.

Thanks again to all my readers, who write from all over the world, criticising, encouraging, praising. Some have been sending me letters since the first *Scottish Football Book* appeared. It's good to know the *Scottish Football Book* has so many friends.

Thanks, too, to the *Evening Times* for their courtesy in allowing me to publish some of the brilliant pictures taken by their photographers in this book.

Well held, sir! Here Alan Rough of Partick Thistle shows why he is Scotland's top goalkeeper

WHEN THE WEMBLEY ROOF FELL IN ...
it was another Disaster for Scotland

Once again the roof fell in on Scotland at Wembley. Once again it was brutal disappointment for the clans who took over London on the Saturday of 26 May, 1979. Once again it was an old familiar story.

The thousands who had travelled south saw their team play England into embarrassed disarray for more than half of the game – and finish with nothing but another defeat to put in the record books.

Once again the banners were sadly put away and the battle songs muted.

And once again Wembley, the ground that has become a graveyard for Scottish international goalkeepers, claimed another victim.

But it started right. With Jock Stein in charge as the new manager, there had been signs against Wales and Ireland that Scotland were entering a new era, fielding a team to play modern, entertaining football and building constructively for the future.

And for Wembley Stein conceived a strategic and tactical approach that worked so well that England might have been buried before the match had run half its course. This involved Kenny Dalglish, the new Scotland captain, being assigned to a much deeper position than he occupies for Liverpool, and only Joe Jordan and Arthur Graham playing up front, which left England with four men at the back marking two forwards.

No wonder the thousands upon thousands of gaily-bedecked, tartan-tammied fans who made Wembley an incredible sea of waving yellow and red banners, a vast choir of Scottish songsters with hardly an Englishman in sight, were in high spirits, despite the dull grey skies and the threatening rain.

All the traditional fire and passion, all the fine fabric that is the Scottish soccer garment was in the team's play as they swarmed on England's goal in the first half, even with the pitch cutting up and the ball skidding, in an atmosphere that seemed to have been specially transported from Hampden Park.

The Scottish hunger for victory was intense. Scotland thundered into the early action with such fervour that it looked as though the English players were outnumbered and the match was less than a quarter of an hour old when a terrible panic fluttered in the hearts of their defence. As Scotland baffled them with intricate passing in the penalty area, Kenny Dalglish and Graeme Souness, that debonair cavalier playing with the flair of a Jim Baxter, were both left holding their heads in dismay as shots were blocked and deflected.

Ray Wilkins stooped to head away a fiendishly curling corner from Dalglish that swirled over and away from keeper Ray Clemence like a feather borne on a whirlwind.

So when Scotland scored in the 21st minute it was a surprise to no one. Scotland had attacked fiercely but intelligently, with Souness displaying a range of invention and delicacy of touch that made us think of gods

8

of the past, with John Wark more than useful and Asa Hartford so convincing.

Stein had sent the players out with a deliberately conceived strategy and the firm conviction that England were in no important sense their superiors and his belief had found validity.

The goal was long overdue indeed. It came when Jordan, having lost the ball, battled stubbornly for re-possession. He did not succeed but the ball did break away from the English defender Neal and into the path of Arthur Graham, a constant aggravation to the English with his close drib-

THE CAVORTING IDIOT . . . that was the skinhead who stopped the England–Scotland international at Wembley for vital first half minutes that some say knocked Scotland out of their stride and caused the overtime in the first half in which England equalised. But who was he? He wore a tartan scarf. Yet Scotland goalkeeper George Wood, one of the players who tried to get rid of the intruder before the English cops finally caught him, said: 'He spoke more like an Englishman than a Scot.'

It remains a mystery. Surprisingly the man who caused so much damage wasn't charged with any offence, merely ejected from the ground.

bling and surges of pace invariably too much for any opponent who took him on one to one.

Graham's cross was struck long and sensibly beyond the far post and when Dalglish artfully guided it back with a cushioned pass John Wark could not fail to accept the gift of an open goal.

So the songs rang out, 'We'll support you ever more,' and all the rest. Scotland, we thought, were on the way.

And then, on the half hour, came an incident which at first seemed funny, an incident from a Keystone Cops comedy. A supporter with a shaven and presumably empty head, bearing aloft a tartan scarf, ran onto the pitch and kept four policemen in frustration for several minutes as he dodged their tackles before he was brought down and dragged away. The boring mindlessness of this action was made even less welcome by the subsequent realization that it had a crucial effect on the outcome of the match.

Jock Stein had come off the Scotland bench to shout fierce advice to the intruder

So near – but yet so far. Arthur Graham is stopped in the nick of time as he makes a menacing raid at Wembley

and the manager was right to assume that such an interruption at that stage could do nothing but harm to the side. It did. It broke Scotland's concentration, stopped the impetus of assault and gave England time to recover.

And worse. The equalizing goal that enabled England so luckily to go in for the interval sighing with relief, was scored in time added on by the referee because of that stupid fan.

Yet in the last 20 minutes of the first half it seemed that discussion about the fan's arrival on the scene of battle would be unnecessary. For Scotland stayed on top, even though their pressure was not so intense, and they had bad luck when fine shots were brilliantly saved by Ray Clemence.

But, after being so close to ecstasy, the Scots were about to suffer one of the traditional disasters that pursue them at Wembley and in those peculiar and vulnerable moments before half-time they lost a shattering goal – well into overtime.

Not a brilliant goal. But a goal that probably won the match for England because it left Scotland dazed and bitter. In cramped space on the edge of the box Keegan fed the ball towards Barnes. Brooking dummied to let it run through. From the Scots point of view it seemed to have arrived in a safe place because Barnes had not managed a memorable gesture let alone a hint of achievement until that time.

What he did was nothing wonderful but the Scottish defenders gave outrageous reward for his efforts. Barnes was allowed to juggle with the ball, turn himself round to face the goal, and then strike a rather slovenly left-foot volley.

Big George Wood, who had been given preference over Alan Rough of Partick Thistle in goal following a capable display against Ireland, was denied a view of the action by colleagues who should have been doing something much more relevant than standing back to watch Barnes's leisurely preparations for the shot. But his response was belated. He lunged to his left but was far too late and found the ball squirming away from his hand and into the net.

That, alas, was the beginning of the end for Scotland. The worst was yet to come.

That goal lifted English hearts and we saw a different team telling another story in the second half.

Although Scotland started as passionately as ever, with more attacking runs by Graham along the right and one marvellous sortie by Hartford and Frankie Gray on the left that was climaxed by a cross from the back that would surely have been exploited by Dalglish had Watson not beaten him to the header, there were signs of incipient disarray in the Scotland defence.

And in 64 minutes the roof fell in on Scotland. A period of prolonged possession by the English came to a point when Mick Mills swung the ball to Wilkins on the right. The midfield man looked offside but no flag rose and Wilkins turned and shot firmly. And the nightmare began for big George Wood. He stopped the ball alright, but couldn't hold it. The ball bounced away – to the foot of Steve Coppell who joyously accepted the gift and put England ahead.

Scotland reeled. And Kevin Keegan, Europe's Player of the Year, took over. What a magnificent goal he scored to make the result 3–1 for England.

By that time, the stands which had throbbed with Scottish battle hymns were silent, the noise slowly but remorselessly throttled as England rolled up their sleeves and fought back.

It was Kevin Keegan who provided his own stunning climax to a remarkable afternoon. He took off with a typical driving run just inside the Scottish half. No Scot could lay a tackle on him. One tried a trip but the Portuguese referee, Antonio Garrido, in vivid red suit, waved play on.

Straight as an arrow, Keegan sped on.

Nice work from Graeme Souness as the Liverpool man clears during an English attack at Wembley

He reached the penalty spot, passed briskly to Brooking, got the ball back and hammered it low inside Wood's left-hand post.

It was a fine goal but what a condemnation of slackness in the Scotland defence.

Scotland lost heart but still tried an attack or two. But Clemence confirmed that

they were losers with a beautiful diving clutch on a cross from Graham.

Why doesn't Scotland have such goalkeepers? That was the sigh of the disconsolate tartan hordes as the final whistle went. The dream had faded and the disaster was fully brought home as we realized the score was: England 3, Scotland 1.

Again it was a dismal day that had started well. An Anglo-Scot on an English paper, Patrick Barclay, summed it up best when he wrote: 'Someone once said that the cruellest method of torturing a Scotsman is to nail his feet to the floor and then play a Jimmy Shand record. The Scots are, however, perfectly capable of devising their own punishment without help from others and the national football team provided a further example at Wembley.

'For the second year in succession, they let England off the hook, condemning those followers who had journeyed to Wembley with the usual boisterous anticipation to an equally familiar feeling of impotence.'

Certainly Scotland can be blamed for losing heart so easily. But what a difference a Tom Forsyth or a David Hay would have made, especially in the spineless second half when Scottish heads drooped, when fast, cocky England contemptuously shrugged aside slack tackles, when all the fight, all the heart went out of the lads in the blue jerseys. But there was no one of the 'tower of strength' type around, with Forsyth of Rangers injured and Hay of Chelsea out of action.

But on the bright side Stein's team is young and only just beginning to develop – a team for the future, with signs already that a fine formula is being evolved.

The eleven at Wembley were:

England: Clemence (Liverpool), Neal (Liverpool), Mills (Ipswich Town), Thomson (Liverpool), Watson (Manchester City), Wilkins (Chelsea), Coppell (Manchester United), Keegan (Hamburg), Latchford (Everton), Brooking (West Ham United), Barnes (Manchester City)
Subs, not used: Corrigan (Manchester City), Sansom (Crystal Palace), Hughes (Liverpool), McDermott (Liverpool), Cunningham (West Bromwich Albion)

Scotland Wood (Everton), Burley (Ipswich Town), Gray (Leeds United), Wark (Ipswich Town), McQueen (Manchester United), Hegarty (Dundee United), Dalglish (Liverpool), Souness (Liverpool), Jordan (Manchester United), Hartford (Manchester City), Graham (Leeds United)
Subs, not used: Rough (Partick Thistle), Narey (Dundee United), Hansen (Liverpool), Munro (St. Mirren), Wallace (Coventry City)

Referee: A. Garrido, Portugal

THE MARATHON FINAL –
and more heartbreak for Hibs

It was the Scottish Cup Final we thought would never end. 'From here to eternity' some wit entitled it. And this marathon between Hibernian and Rangers went on and on and on.

Indeed, it lasted 330 minutes before there was a decision.

And when it did end we were sorry. For the third close encounter was a magnificent advertisement for Scottish football.

The match, played on Monday night, 28 May 1979, at Hampden, following two draws, had drama and excitement, triumph and heartbreak, silken Scottish soccer skills and pulsating physical contact.

And it had – at last – goals.

In short, it was a tapestry of all that is good in our game.

Few people outside Edinburgh gave Hibernian a chance in the 1979 Cup Final. One reason was the poor record of the Easter Road club in Scotland's premier knock-out competition. Although Hibs once presented the most dazzling eleven in football, the Famous Five who will never be forgotten and who made their club supreme at one time in the First Division, they hadn't won the Cup since 1902. Since then, when Hibernian beat Celtic (and at Celtic Park, too) 1–0 in the final to win the trophy for the only time in their history, it had been one disaster after another.

Six times Hibs played in the final – to finish beaten runners-up on every occasion. And that was why they were 4–1 underdogs with Rangers hot favourites.

One man, however, had faith in his young team – manager Eddie Turnbull, who had been a member of that Famous Five side of just after the war.

He considered his lads were again on the verge of greatness. And he was confident they would upset Rangers.

Turnbull was right.

The first stanza of the long drawn out final was played on 12 May at Hampden, with a crowd of only 50,610 watching.

It was disappointing, only coming to life in the last 15 minutes. Rangers were in command but lacked punch, despite splendid play by winger David Cooper. But Hibs played shrewdly and they had a hero in goalkeeper Jim McArthur. They were content to let Rangers attack all out and then hit on the break.

The next episode in the marathon was more exciting. This time it went to extra time. But still it was deadlock.

Most people were starting to yawn. Would the final go on until next season? Would it never end?

The third and final chapter made up for all the disappointment. The patience of the fans who had turned up for the previous two games was rewarded.

This time Hibs travelled from Edinburgh full of enthusiasm and commitment and Rangers, who had surrendered the Premier

A swift tackle by Rangers' Colin Jackson robs Hibs' Ally Brazil of a chance in the Scottish Cup Final at Hampden

League title to Celtic and who had to win the final to ensure a place in a top European tournament, had a touch of nerves.

The deadlock which had persisted throughout 16 days and three and a half hours of actual football was broken 16 minutes into the second replay. It was Hibs who scored – and Hibs who deserved to.

Ally McLeod, that skilful manipulator of the midfield, had spread passes across Hampden which upset Rangers to the point of distraction. And Hibs were playing fine football, football that reminded their sup-

porters in the 30,000 crowd who had braved the rain, of their Famous Five and the days of soccer's wine and roses at Easter Road.

The goal came at the end of a quick one-touch move started by Arthur Duncan, a distinguished, speedy left-winger who had done well in a new career at left back but a man who was to end the match so sadly.

But here was a moment of delirious hap-

15

piness for Duncan. His fine crossfield ball found the bustling Gordon Rae, who touched on to striker Colin Campbell. Again, in this splendid move, the ball went back to Rae. He shot. Goalkeeper Peter McCloy couldn't hold the ball. And Tony Higgins arrived for the rebound and trundled the ball over the line.

Hibs deserved their lead and with lively centre forward Campbell twice dragging shots just wide within a minute, the outsiders served notice that they intended to claim the Cup. And favourites Rangers were suffering all kinds of problems.

Their frustration showed in the booking of Derek Parlane for a foul on centre half George Stewart who was in complete command – and their desperation was clear when they threw captain Derek Johnstone, who had been kept back in defence, into the striking role to try to ensure that the previous week's failure to win the League was not followed by Cup defeat.

But how this move paid off for Rangers! And for poor Hibs it was like Scotland at Wembley the Saturday before.

Their build-ups were well-planned. Their raids were searing. But, like Scotland at Wembley, they couldn't add to their lead.

And then, as happened to goalkeeper George Wood against England, tragedy struck Hibs goalie Jim McArthur, who had played so brilliantly, just three minutes from the interval.

True, wee Tommy McLean, back to his best form, did exceedingly well to escape the clutches of the powerful Hibs defenders, and coolly trot upfield with the ball before unleashing a shot.

It was no thunderbolt, though. It didn't

Arthur Duncan, a hit for Hibs at left back

matter. McArthur allowed the greasy ball to squirm from his grip and there was Derek Johnstone – just as Steve Coppell had been for England's second goal in the international – in the right place to tap the ball in for the equaliser.

That was all Rangers needed. It had been a master stroke to push Johnstone forward. And so the second half belonged to Rangers.

They had recovered their poise. Young Robert Russell took over from McLeod as the brain and turned his team into the dream machine of earlier in the season with a contribution of accurate passes and ability to float into the open spaces.

Hibs appeared to be down and out when Derek Johnstone inevitably put Rangers ahead in 61 minutes.

And that was a goal fit to win any final. For the big Ranger devastatingly hooked a Russell knee-high cross past the helpless McArthur.

And then it was that Hibs rose to the occasion again. Their tradition, their pride in their club, came to their tiring players' rescue. Somehow they hit back and when Bobby Hutchison came on for Higgins they equalised.

The substitute in his first foray was pulled down by Colin Jackson. A penalty, said referee Ian Foote, though it looked soft. That didn't worry Ally McLeod who pulled the match out of the fire for Hibs by equalising from the spot.

And so to extra time – once again. And the drama continued, the excitement mounted and there was fine football to leave the fans breathless.

It was a final to remember indeed.

There were now heroics by keeper McArthur to make up for his first half boob – a marvellous save from Alex Miller when the Rangers substitute (who came on for

Non-stop Des Bremner, dynamic Hibernian midfield man

Hibs keeper Jim McArthur in action, with Rangers' Billy Urquhart storming in

Tommy McLean) took a penalty which was even softer than that awarded to Hibs, Parlane appearing to fall after a tackle.

But there was heartbreak for Arthur Duncan in the 319th minute of the everlasting final when he headed past his own keeper after David Cooper had dazzled on the wing and sent over a venomous cross.

Duncan could hardly be blamed. The cross was a harbinger of doom for the Edinburgh side, who had fought so gallantly – a cross that carried all the menace of a dive bomber, so accurately flighted was it.

Duncan could only take a flying, desperate, despairing leap. For if he hadn't tried to get to the ball first, a posse of Rangers were jumping in to make sure. And that was the winner.

So Rangers won the Cup, to add to the League Cup already in their cupboard. They won the honour that took them into the European Cup Winners' Cup mainly because of the brilliant play of Robert Russell, named man of the match, the magic footwork of Cooper and the storming assaults of Johnstone when he was moved up front.

Yet there was great sympathy for Hibs, who went so near to landing the Cup that has eluded them for 77 years. It all ended in heartbreak again. But Eddie Turnbull was not despondent. 'Our youngsters can only mature all the quicker because of that great display,' he said.

And certainly Hibs looked like a team who are on the way back to the form and style which once made them the pride of Scottish football.

The teams in the marathon record final were:

12 May – *Rangers*: McCloy, Jardine, Dawson, Johnstone, Jackson, MacDonald, McLean, Russell, Parlane, Smith, Cooper
Subs: Miller, Urquhart
Hibs: McArthur, Brazil, Duncan, Bremner, Stewart, McNamara, Hutchison, McLeod, Campbell, Callachan, Higgins
Subs: Brown, Rae
Referee: B. R. McGinlay, Glasgow

16 May – *Rangers*: McCloy, Jardine, Dawson, Johnstone, Jackson, MacDonald, McLean, Russell, Parlane, Smith, Cooper
Subs: Miller, Urquhart
Hibs: McArthur, Brazil, Duncan, Bremner, Stewart, McNamara, Rae, McLeod, Campbell, Callachan, Higgins
Subs: Brown, Hutchison
Referee: B. R. McGinlay, Glasgow

28 May – *Rangers*: McCloy, Jardine, Dawson, Johnstone, Jackson, Watson, McLean, Russell, Parlane, MacDonald, Cooper
Subs: Smith, Miller
Hibs: McArthur, Brazil, Duncan, Bremner, Stewart, McNamara, Rae, McLeod, Campbell, Callachan, Higgins
Subs: Brown, Hutchison
Referee: Ian Foote, Glasgow

A QUESTION OF FLAIR

Thankfully, method football is on the way out. It paid dividends in the way of results. But it never did much for the game and groans go up when you mention Catenaccio or Ramsey's Wingless Wonders.

Certainly it was never accepted in Scotland. For in this country the artist was always king. Dour, faceless, all-purpose players may have played a part, but they were never applauded.

The hero was always the inside forward with the master's touch, the silky half back with his velvety passing, the tricky wee winger who made defenders blush. In short, the player with flair.

And once again it's flair that is counting in Scottish soccer. Once again this little country is producing players who wear the mantle of magic, who have that air of arrogance the fans love, and who delight in the off-beat move, the bewildering feint, the slick change of pace and position – players who want to play real football, to win by sheer skill alone, to pull off the unusual . . . to bring flair to football.

Now meet two of the lads who are becoming the new Alex James, the new Jim Baxters, aye, even the new Andy Patons of soccer. . . .

Centre half with a difference

Alan Hansen, late of Partick Thistle and now of Liverpool, is the accomplished young player who is likely to bear most responsibility in Scotland's international team in the future. On his broad shoulders manager Jock Stein puts the task of bringing a new dimension to our football. Out, in the manager's opinion, is the stopper centre half. In is the central defender who can play football, who will play his part in building up attacks. Hansen is the great young Scot who can best fit into that role.

It was only last season that he emerged into the top class, winning his place in Liverpool's first team and becoming the new type of Scotland defender Stein relishes.

Liverpool signed him from Partick Thistle for £100,000 in May 1977 and he quickly fitted into the Anfield set-up. That was no surprise because Alan Hansen is blessed with considerable mental ability, undeniable good looks and a rare diversity of athletic talents, for he is far better than average in many other sports too and would surely have represented his country at golf if he hadn't made soccer his main aim.

Alan has A-levels in history, English, mathematics and Latin and his unorthodoxy is not confined to his academic qualifications. He has turned into a new type of centre half, the Beckenbauer type of slick artist who relies more on well-read interceptions than on tackles and whose ambition it is to build a swift attack by a pass or a foray that would be envied by a Baxter.

He doesn't, of course, look like the kind of No. 5 who is usually built on Clydesdale lines. He is tall but thin and elegant rather than robust.

Alan sees himself as 'a thinking

Paul Sturrock of Dundee United

defender,' and that's the right phrase. 'I'm the kind who likes to play football,' he says. 'I don't just like to clear the ball into the terraces. I like to hold it and do something positive.' Which is, of course, just what Jock Stein wants him to do.

He grins when he remembers what his manager Bob Paisley, a down-to-earth character who loves the way his new boy plays but has no time for fripperies that are over fancy, said to him when he started in Liverpool's first team. 'I guess I was just too cocky at times,' says Alan, 'but the boss soon let me know that I was playing for the greatest team in Britain not for myself and, although I've made a few mistakes, mainly

positional by the way, I reckon my play is a lot better now.

'I like to think I can read the game quite well. Anyhow, mine is the easiest position to play. You can see everything that's happening up front.'

At Anfield his mate is the magnificent Kenny Dalglish, toast of the Kop. 'I've got to go around a lot with Kenny,' laughs Alan. 'He's my chauffeur. I've failed my driving test three times. But Kenny lives round the corner from me so I go home with him.'

Life is great for Alan Hansen and we look forward to seeing him displaying his varied and sometimes unusual skills in the blue of Scotland for a long time.

Curiously, Alan Hansen could have been signed by Liverpool – for nothing. As a 15 year old he was on trial at Anfield, playing in practice matches and taking part in training. But when he returned home he received a letter from the then manager, Bill Shankly, which said, in effect, that he wouldn't measure up to Liverpool standards!

He doesn't get much golf now and, indeed, football is his only love. But he could be a natural at whatever sport he cared to turn to. He has represented Scotland at volleyball and golf, but it will be as a great Scotland footballer that Alan Hansen will be remembered.

Brave new breed

Talk about football flair and at once Dundee United springs to mind. No one finds rare young talent and moulds it into star material better than manager Jim McLean. And flair is the real secret of the success of the Tannadice club. They have, indeed,

Alan Hansen, so suave, so elegant, in action for Liverpool. Also in the picture is Willie Donachie, Manchester City's Scottish international back

probably more players with the touch of glamour than any other Scottish club – Dave Narey, Paul Hegarty, Ray Stewart, Graeme Payne and Paul Sturrock. They're a brave new breed.

And reaching his peak as a player of major talent is Sturrock, lean and hungry attacker, in the words of his manager, 'a positive player.'

Paul, a railwayman's son, was brought up in picturesque Pitlochry, more famous for its scenery than for football. He had a footballing background, though, as his father, George, played for Highland League clubs Peterhead and Deveronvale.

His career started the day a Perthshire amateur side found themselves short of a player and discovered a centre forward who took positive delight in putting the ball in the net.

From that day on Paul was football daft. He scored seventy-two goals in a memorable season for the local Vale of Atholl side. Then he signed for Bankfoot Juniors, the Perthshire Junior club. It was there that he was spotted by the astute Jim McLean and the Dundee United manager got in just in time for a host of other big teams were after Paul, including Manchester City.

That was in 1973. Jim McLean's first task was to tell the youngster that he had to give up one of his superstitions – that he could only play well if his hair was shoulder length and worn with a head-band!

Sturrock, now on the verge of full international honours, is one of those nippy yet artistic players the fans love to watch. His manager explains: 'Paul is unbelievably sharp at changing direction and his other great asset is that he always wants to get in behind opposing defences. He has shown how good he is with the Scotland Under-21 team and he must go right to the top.'

And if it's flair you're after, you can't rule out Sturrock's team-mate, David Narey. Call David the Complete Footballer, for he shows artistry and know-how whether he's at the back, in the middle or even up front, though most people believe he is at his best when paired at centre back with the equally talented Paul Hegarty.

Alan Hansen signs for Liverpool, watched by manager Bob Paisley

WHAT'S THIS ALL ABOUT, THEN?

Children at a school near Ibrox went to work with a will when Rangers asked them to help clear the snow from the pitch to allow the European Cup-tie with Cologne to go on. This fine picture – revealing what a blow the Siberian weather struck at football – is by Robin Gray, *Evening Times* photographer

Left: That's what the foul was for, says star referee Brian McGinlay. But Hearts players Jim Jefferies and Frank Liddell don't appear to agree with him, despite his knees-up demonstration

Right: A sight St Mirren fans won't see this season. For Frank McGarvey, celebrating a great goal, has been transferred to Liverpool

Football is a lonely game...

... for this Rangers fan, at least. But even though he is all on his own, he's enjoying himself. And he's cheering a fine goal scored by his favourite player, Robert Russell.

What's it all about?

This supporter is guarding the vast, empty terracing where Rangers are erecting a new grandstand at Ibrox.

He won't be on his own this season when Ibrox will become one of the most modern and comfortable stadia in the country.

THIRD TIME LUCKY
by Jim Murphy, Dundee FC

Saturday, 23 December 1978, proved to me that you can be lucky third time round in football.

That was the day I made my Dundee debut as a substitute in the last 30 minutes of the First Division match against Airdrie at Broomfield.

And I had been on the field only five or 10 minutes when I became the happiest player in Scottish football and realized that the game was worth playing after all.

A long clearance out of defence landed just inside our own half and Billy Pirie hooked it on. I ran into the Airdrie half, just beating one of their players to the ball and suddenly I was right through on Ernie McGarr.

The keeper came out and as he did so I curled a right-foot shot around him into the net. The goal gave Dundee a 2–0 win that was important in the promotion battle and it gave me the biggest thrill of my life. At last I felt I had made the grade.

I didn't know it then but I would have to wait what seemed a lifetime for my chance to prove to the Dundee fans that I had something to offer the side that was going for promotion.

Because of the big freeze that brought Scottish football to an almost total halt last season, it was eight weeks before Dundee kicked another ball.

I can tell you that those eight weeks dragged like nothing else I have ever known. There I was desperate to get on with the game and, week in, week out, I was told when I telephoned the park, 'Sorry, but the game is off again.'

As you can appreciate, the long wait didn't do a lot for the confidence I had gained from scoring that goal in my debut at Airdrie.

But eventually, on 21 February 1979, I was finally told that we would be back in action against Clydebank in an important promotion match at Dens Park.

It was a game we had to win to stay with the leaders after so long out of action. Manager Tommy Gemmell knew just how important it was to the side but he didn't forget that it was also important to me individually. Before the game, he gave the word in the dressing-room that if we kicked off the ball should go to me right away so that I would get an early touch and perhaps do something with it that would help my confidence.

I don't think even the boss knew that the move would pay such a handsome dividend. We did kick off, I did get the ball, and within a minute of the start we were a goal up.

I made a good run down the right wing, beating a couple of men, and a Clydebank defender had to concede a corner as he stopped me from going in on goal or making the cross. I took the kick myself and Ian Redford put the ball in the net. I could hardly believe it and suddenly the worries that had piled up during that eight-week wait were gone.

We went on to win the match 2–1 – an

Jim Murphy of Dundee

important step towards returning to the Premier League after three years in the First Division.

For a spell after that I just couldn't do anything wrong. In our next game, against Falkirk in the Scottish Cup, I was pulled down in the penalty area and Billy Pirie scored from the spot to give us a 1–0 win.

That set us up for our best game of all the season. We played St Mirren off the park in the next round for a 4–1 win that even our biggest fans found hard to believe.

That cup-tie gave the players a tremendous lift because it proved to us all that we could live with a top Premier League side if we gave one hundred per cent. And I think it helped us a lot later in the season when we were fighting for promotion.

By the time we finally did gather enough points to make certain of going up, I wasn't sure of my regular place in the first team. The boss wanted a different approach away from home at times so that I found myself on the subs bench pretty regularly.

I didn't mind that too much because I felt that I had contributed something. And it was certainly a lot better than some of the experiences I had had earlier in my career.

When I was sixteen and playing for my school team, Holy Cross, I had been spotted by Celtic and eventually signed by them. For my first season I was farmed out to Bellshill Athletic and then I thought I had really made it when I was called up at the start of the next season as a full time player.

Things seemed to be going really well for me, too, in that season at Parkhead. I went on tour with the first team to Ireland, played for them in the national five-a-side tournament at Wembley and even replaced Kenny Dalglish during a testimonial game.

I felt I was on the way to making it as a full time player. So you can imagine my shock and hurt when I was told at the end of the season that I was being freed by Celtic.

The blow was softened somewhat when I was asked to join Queen of the South and found myself getting a game fairly regularly in the first team. But by the end of the season I was playing in the reserve side at Dumfries ... a reserve side that was scrapped because of financial cut-backs by the club.

So once again I found myself on the heap, out of football. And this time I decided to stay out. I made up my mind that I would make my money from being a window cleaner in the family business.

And that is what I did for the next eighteen months, quite content to have turned my back on the game. Then I started getting telephone calls from John Phillips and Pat Docherty, who ran Bellshill, trying to persuade me to return to the game as a junior. Eventually, because they were stuck for a Scottish Cup-tie against Arniston Rangers through injuries, I said I would give it a go. But I made it clear that I would make no promises about playing more than the one game.

However, I scored the only goal of the match and rediscovered my appetite for football. Before long I was playing for the Central Region representative side and also for Scotland Juniors.

It was then that I heard whispers about Dundee being interested and I learned that they were having me watched in a District match against Tayside in Dundee. I scored a goal in the game, got myself voted man of the match, and suddenly my career took off again.

Before I knew it, I had played a couple of trials, impressed, and put pen to paper to become a Dens Park player.

I started as a full-timer on Monday, 18 December and by the Saturday I was making that first appearance as a substitute at Airdrie ... proving to myself that everything comes right in the end if you are prepared to wait for the third time to come around.

33

EVANS – Star Rebel left with Memories

It is a futile but nevertheless fascinating exercise to look back in football and wonder how many of the magnificent players we knew all those years ago would have been stars in the more determined, more method-based and probably crisper, faster and more intense soccer of today.

Some, alas, and it grieves me to say so, would have failed. But many would be just as outstanding in the modern game as they were in the 1950s.

And a few would have outshone the last World Cup stars. They were superb players, splendid internationalists, the toast of their countries and their clubs, idolized by thousands.

Certainly Bobby Evans, of Celtic and Scotland, would have been a million pound player today. He had everything to make him great in the years after the war. His style, enthusiasm and skill and his power and stamina would have had the top managers in the world today drooling. Bobby Evans would have fitted perfectly into the total football scene of 1979.

His flaming hair a symbol of inspiration, his work-rate incredible, his reading of play impeccable, Bobby was every schoolboy's hero – Mr Perpetual Motion. He was a combination of the powerful and the artistic, a player who would have been just right for the midfield of World Cup holders Argentina.

Captain of Celtic and Scotland, much travelled with caps galore, he was a top professional for more than twenty years.

What player in Britain, you would have thought, had more going for him in soccer.

But although Bobby Evans may have been as much at home in a modern soccer set-up as he was long ago, he would notice a big difference in footballers' life styles. Unlike the glittering stars of today, there was no thousand pounds a week, no Jaguar in the drive of a country mansion, no race-horse in the paddock. Football didn't make many of the big names of yesterday rich.

And these days, Bobby Evans, who finished playing just over ten years ago, is just an ordinary bloke battling to beat the rising cost of living, his days of glamour merely a memory.

He's a storeman and sometimes a van driver with a firm near his home in East Kilbride. He says: 'I haven't a great deal of spare time for I work late two nights a week and on Sunday mornings.'

He isn't, however, a moaner, isn't envious of today's stars who walk so proudly on football's golden mile. He isn't complaining about his lot because he's happy with his life in the new town of East Kilbride.

Bobby had a serious illness which almost finished him five years ago so he has learned to take things as they come. He recalls: 'It was a humbling experience, especially after such an active career as mine. I moved from hospital to hospital and ended up in a wheelchair for a spell.'

Is he bitter and jealous of today's big money players? 'Not a bit of it,' he says.

This is Bobby Evans as he was at the height of his fame with Celtic and Scotland

'Good luck to the lads who are now being paid what they're worth, considering the crowds they pull in, in England, anyhow.

'As for me, I shall be eternally grateful that I have been nursed back to fitness again. Perhaps I felt more folk would have come to see me in hospital if my illness had happened only a few years before – the ward would have been packed. But now I'm grateful if someone stops me in the street and asks me for my autograph.'

With a smile, he recalls that he was always something of a rebel, though a likeable one. If he had paid more obeisance to the establishment, might he not still be a big shot in football?

'I don't think so,' he said. 'Anyhow, how could I? I always had to say what I thought was right.'

And Bobby remembered how as a fiery redhead he told the SFA he didn't want to be considered for any further caps for Scotland following a dispute; how he had a blazing row with team manager Andy Beattie after a defeat by Austria, claiming that man-for-man marking had been wrong for the occasion; how, in the World Cup of 1958 in Sweden, he was in bother when he locked himself in a bedroom instead of travelling with the Scottish party to watch another of the ties. As a result he was almost sent home.

Most sensational of all was his fall-out with Celtic, the club he served so brilliantly for sixteen years after signing from St Anthony's as a teenager in 1945. He shook Celtic and all of football by asking for a transfer. He got it, too, and was sold to Chelsea.

How does he feel about that now? The parting still rankles but Evans refuses to elaborate on the reason other than that he was made a promise he feels the club did not mean to keep. And he adds: 'I always believed in speaking my mind. I'd do the same again.'

Certainly no one spoke up like Bobby Evans. I know that alright. If I wrote something he didn't like, he wasn't long in telling me. No one, though, could ever doubt that Bobby always stuck up for what he thought was right.

Neither could anyone doubt that Evans – a lifelong non-drinker and non-smoker and a superb trainer – was a world class footballer who played more than a full part in winning games for Celtic and Scotland.

He won forty-eight full international caps for Scotland and was twice captain against England.

One thing he can't understand is that currently testimonial matches are becoming almost as regular as ordinary matches. 'Why are they generally played for those who are not really in need of money?' he wonders – and that's a question more than a few people are asking.

After a year with Chelsea, Evans lived up to his Welsh-sounding name by joining Newport County. Then he returned north to Morton, became player-manager of Third Lanark and finished up with Raith Rovers at the age of forty.

He feels that one of the best Celtic teams of all time was the 1953-54 line up when a peak was reached and the Scottish Cup won. But few of that star-studded team ever found wealth or knew about the film star salaries today's soccer heroes receive. Jock Stein is manager of Scotland, Sean Fallon is now a director at Dumbarton, Bertie Peacock runs a pub in Northern Ireland, Willie Fernie drives a taxi, Neilly Mochan is Celtic trainer.

Sadly, few players of yesteryear enjoy the riches which fall to stars of today.

But Bobby Evans says he's a lucky man, happy with the way things are. He's still interested in football and goes along to see Morton when he takes the notion. 'It's still a great game and in spite of everything I've many super memories,' he says.

And so has the football public of Bobby Evans!

BE KIND TO THE REFEREE – He's One Man against the World

Let's be kinder to the poor old referee!

That's my plea as criticism of the competence of match officials mounts in newspapers and on radio and television. The referees feel they are being treated unfairly by the media, especially television. And not only is this the case in Scotland. All over the world referees are taking more and more stick.

Indeed, at a recent UEFA referees course

WHO'D BE A REFEREE

Often a referee's lot is not a happy one – for footballers aren't the easiest of athletes to control, especially when they think they've been wronged.

But the good referee stands no nonsense, as the pictures throughout this chapter show.

No way I'm changing my mind, says referee Bill Anderson as Aberdeen players protest after he has awarded a penalty to Rangers

Few players tried to argue with Tiny Wharton, one of our biggest and best referees. Here is Tom Wharton breaking up a row between Rangers and Celtic players

held in Vienna, a talk was given on the subject 'The media and us' by West German officials, who are gravely concerned at the criticism.

This was the salient point: 'The referee is the most important member of football's supporting cast but should remain as inconspicuous as possible during a match. But this is becoming increasingly difficult. Now the referee is observed too closely, his every movement checked by thousands of people on the terraces and hundreds more in the press and commentary boxes. It was not always so but presumably nobody ever thought of making the man in the middle the centre of attention as he so often is today.'

What's gone wrong? There is a feeling in Scotland that there are no new Jack Mowats, no new Peter Craigmyles, or Tiny Whartons or Bobby Davidsons, that refereeing standards have slipped.

For the spectator, the referee will always be a mixture of bogeyman and pantaloon – an old-fashioned dominie spoiling the fun, a Saturday substitute for traffic wardens, bosses or even husbands and wives, a figure easily abused.

For the player too, many referees have become a mere book-keeper, his powers of discretion replaced by yellow and red cards, his scope limited by the knowledge that he is being judged from the stands by supervisors who will award marks for his performance and downgrade him if he doesn't hand out the statutory punishments.

Another great and stern referee was Bobby Davidson, now an Airdrie director. He is having a few anything-but-kind words with John Blackley of Hibs and Newcastle United

One manager summed it up to me like this: 'I know referees have a difficult job but they are now told to put a stress on certain aspects of the game and some have taken this far too literally. I think there should be more feeling for the situation of the professional. The referee should relax a little bit more and if he's fit and up with the game then a wee word in the ear can sometimes save unpleasantness later on.'

Still the referees feel they are being hard done by. And certainly we don't realize just what uninhibited enthusiasm referees show for football, just how much time they spend at their associations and groups in discussing ways in which it can be improved, just what strength of devotion enables referees to travel long distances to drab little towns for small fees.

We don't realize, either, that refereeing has become more difficult because of the increased speed at which the game is played, the ball flying from one end of the field to the other in a series of adroit movements – much more difficult indeed than it was a quarter or a century ago when styles were more sedate.

As one official said ruefully: 'Spotting fouls can be as difficult as catching pickpockets on Derby Day. In an instant we have to decide whether the foul was intentional or whether it was simply a tackle mistimed. Of course, we all make mistakes. Every one of us has known the stomach-tightening sensation of having to stick to a decision which he knows is wrong the moment after he has made it.'

That's true – but who makes allowances for it? I should know. It happens to reporters and commentators as well. Only the other day, Denis Law, now a writer and television commentator, said: 'I remember thinking what a so-and-so you were when you were reporting some of the games in which I played. I know better now that I've got to do it. The fact is that a pressman – and a referee – has to make up his mind in

a matter of seconds on a decision that would take a High Court judge a month to ponder.'

So referees are entitled to feel aggrieved if they are continually subjected to criticism which does not take these human factors into account.

How, then, can the referee play his part in promoting a good public image? Here are some of the ways suggested in the talks at the Vienna Congress.

Try as he may, the referee, who is on the field neither to score goals nor to save them but merely to ensure that the game is played according to the rules, is today less successful in remaining as inconspicuous as he should.

For every referee finds himself up against several groups of people at once – the twenty-two players, the spectators and the media representatives. They will all be hard in their judgement of his performance. Players will try to win an advantage through hidden fouls or theatrical forms of deception. Spectators try to unnerve the referee by booing, whistling and shouting all kinds of abuse. Match commentators study the vital incidents again before passing their remarks. They are all often unsparing in their judgement of the referee.

Once the referee had it much easier. No doubt players and spectators at that time became just as incensed by an unfavourable decision as they do today. But the difference is that nowadays the critics all feel they are backed up in their opinions by slow-motion repeats of vital scenes on television, providing them with the proof (or what they think is the proof) they are looking for. Then the same old argument flares up all over again about whether *de facto* decisions should still

And sometimes the poor old ref takes a knock. Celtic physio Bob Rooney gives referee John Paterson, who strained a muscle, a helping hand at Parkhead

remain irrevocable even when films or other electronic evidence is available.

(Incidentally, I read a lovely letter in one of the quality newspapers which said the referee should have the same facilities as the television commentators and be given a chance to watch the replay before making up his mind. What the writer didn't say was how the poor old ref was to see the slow-motion repeat. Presumably he would have to carry a portable television set on his back, then hold up play until he had decided what had really happened!)

The referee congress also heard a point of view which intrigues us in Scotland, where referees aren't allowed to talk about their decisions: 'For decades, it was a studiously observed principle in most national football associations to shield the referee from public discussion as much as possible. It may have been right to take this attitude and perhaps it still is. The referee should not become involved in controversies for it would jeopardize the essential authority of his position if he were to end up having to justify his decisions to clubs, players or the public. So far, so good.

'But there are many instances where criticism of the referee can be defused or averted by a word of explanation at the right moment. But cutting the referee off from the media or the public completely means that the official and the authorities are depriving themselves of the chance of making a rational and measured presentation of their own point of view. This refers, of course, not to personal publicity but to the opportunity to give the public a correct and accurate impression of the referee as a human being, who may make mistakes and who certainly cannot have the same precision of vision as a slow-motion camera and yet who still deserves to have the public's confidence.

'Everybody today goes in for public relations. So why shouldn't referees follow suit?

'We should all stop and think in the face of the modern fans who are always ready to take up the chant accusing the referee of partiality or of fixing a match.

'What can be done to rid refereeing of this unwarranted bad reputation? Well, referees have nothing to hide and no aspect of refereeing need be protected from critical observation. Top referees who have been especially well prepared for their duties can and should be made familiar to the public off the field of play as well as on it.

'A referee should not have to defend the decisions he has taken during a game. It is usually enough for him to point out that he has seen a particular incident from a different angle from the spectators or the critics in the stand or that he has had to make a decision quickly and unerringly.

'The referee's sense of justice is not in question. It is rather the sense of justice of the spectators and of certain pressmen which is deficient. Clubs, managers and the mass media should all give thought to how spectators could be taught that the most important thing is not to gain advantage at all costs and an effort should be made to uphold the principles of fairness and justice in the football stadiums of the world.'

There you are then. Obviously, the referees are worried, feeling they are being unfairly criticized. So I repeat – why not try to be kinder to the referee?

Although the referees should ask themselves why the authorities have felt it necessary to standardize the control of games and whether more can be done to improve the overall consistency in dealing with offences . . . and remember that a wee word in the ear is far more sensible than a dramatic pulling out of a notebook.

THE MAN WHO HAD EVERYTHING

The second time around may show that a player verging on the age of thirty will indeed achieve his ambition and become the new Gordon Smith.

Ten years ago Peter Marinello was the winger who had everything. Like the great Gordon Smith he was playing for Hibernian. Like Gordon, too, his play was nicely muted and you felt when watching this brilliant young winger that he had never any need to stamp on the loud pedal, to pelt at full gallop down the wing. He had the gift of ball control and he could shoot accurately and venomously. Like Smith all those years ago, this most graceful of wingers made us feel that style was all. He was poetry in motion. His rippling rhythm brought a glimpse of true art to a game which is all too often a shoddy exercise by players who are not even skilled journeymen. The world seemed to be at those twinkling feet.

In 1969 he was transferred to Arsenal for the then huge fee of £100,000. And Peter received the star treatment. He had his own agent. He wrote a newspaper column. He was idolized by the fans. You could see him on a twenty-foot advertising hoarding.

Peter Marinello seemed destined to become the most glamorous, perhaps the greatest, Scottish footballer to star in the English capital, the city that became the home of some of the most famous players from north of the border – James, Jackson, Gallacher among them.

But it all went wrong. Why? Says Marinello with a sigh: 'I suppose the thing you learn about life is that nothing comes to you at exactly the right time. You can't turn a knob and get exactly what you want just when you want it.

'My first year at Highbury was just too much for me. After all, I had only a year's experience at Easter Road and I couldn't cope with all the glamour of Arsenal.

'It's so obvious now that all those things came to me too quickly when I joined Arsenal. I had so much to learn about football and I certainly had no right modelling clothes, writing columns and having voice tests for records. It's not surprising that some of the Arsenal players got the needle with me. There I was, nineteen years old, just a year into the game and getting all that cream and they were looking at me and saying: "OK, so what's so special about you?" '

What was so special about Peter Marinello was not the turn of speed and the tricky footwork. It was the dark hair and the winsome looks and the belief that he could do for London what George Best was doing for Manchester.

And at Highbury Peter felt manager Bertie Mee and the coaching staff were treating him as an ornament.

'The big trouble,' he said, 'was that the Arsenal team were beginning to do well in their style, which relied heavily on teamwork rather than on individual flair. I found I was being used for games where a bit of individual work on the wings helped the

Peter Marinello, the player who is starting
all over again

side's image. But when the big matches came, the finals of competitions, I was left out.

'Anyhow, I was so under-developed it wasn't true. I was believing my own publicity. I didn't realize that I was a commodity rather than a footballer. I hadn't created anything for myself.

'Perhaps, looking back, I feel I should have soldiered on a bit longer with Arsenal but when I was dropped just before a semi-final, I thought, "Here we go again, another cup final coming up and I'm getting the elbow." '

In his three years with Arsenal, Marinello had only fifty-seven competitive games. So he elected to travel for a second £100,000, this time to Portsmouth.

But again he failed to fulfil his potential. There were few bells chiming for him at Pompey as the club was practically on the rocks and after two and a half years he was glad to get away.

'That,' he reflects, 'was a mistake, though I liked the club.'

So it was back to Scotland and Motherwell, where it appeared he would pass the remainder of his football career, still feeling himself to be unfulfilled as an artist, his splendid gifts never really utilized.

Although he was chosen for the Scottish League for the match against Ireland, Peter seldom showed more than a few glimpses of his extraordinary skill and seemed fated to be just another youngster who flattered, as they say, to deceive.

One man, however, had faith in Marinello, believed he could still become a Gordon Smith. That was Fulham manager Bobby Campbell and in late 1978 he brought him back south. Almost at once Peter made the impact and, at the second time around, he looks like at last becoming the toast of a London crowd.

The Marinello story points a moral to aspiring youngsters inclined to believe that a change is usually for the good. But, chuckles Peter, 'There is one good thing about moving – it's a funny thing but when you get around in this game you do make money. And when you are moving you always go for a bigger house.'

He adds seriously: 'I suppose getting back to Scotland was my salvation. Doing a bit for Motherwell helped me get back some self-respect, though I have to say I never let myself go in England. I suppose deep down I felt a failure when I went back to Scotland.'

Why did he take the decision to chance his legs once more in the London area? Pride, undoubtedly. Another opportunity to prove himself. 'Ten years,' he murmured, 'is a long time to live with being a failed superstar. Especially when you have known, all the time, that you could play a bit.'

Now Peter, his choirboy face belying his near thirty years, is convinced he can become as good as his idol, Gordon Smith – and in London.

And he believes it won't be a case of people saying he was the player who had everything – but the player who *has* everything.

It wasn't however, until he had gone back to London that Marinello helped to clear up a mystery which had puzzled Scottish fans. Why was his new form with Fulham so rarely seen when he was with Motherwell?

Peter explains it like this – and makes a point which caused dispute in Scotland last season and with which so many people agree: 'It is because the tackle from behind is outlawed in England. There's a world of difference between playing as a forward in Scotland and England. You get time to hold the ball in England and you are not looking over your shoulder for lunging tackles all the time.'

Peter feels referees give forwards far more protection in England. 'How often,' he asks, 'do the crowd see a forward actually run

A flash of Marinello as he shines for the Scottish League against the Irish League at Fir Park

with the ball in Scotland now, yet it used to be one of the great characteristics of our game. I just don't think it's on for a player in Scotland to make that sort of move any more. If a defender whacks you from the back in Scottish League games the play is usually allowed to go on but it's stopped in England.'

Perhaps it's time that in Scotland there was an instruction to tighten up on defenders who tackle so fiercely from behind. That would make the game better for the fans to watch.

OH, THOSE MEMORABLE FOOTBALL YEARS – a Quarter of a Century of Triumph and Tragedy

In this edition, *The Scottish Football Book* reaches its quarter century. Twenty-five years of Scottish soccer – it's a long time. And certainly there have been changes in the game: new methods, new styles, new ideas, alas, smaller crowds, perhaps less entertainment.

But football survives. It is still the greatest game in the world. And there is one unchanging aspect of Scottish football – the fan. He is still the keenest, the man on the

Yes, football's all about triumph and tragedy. And what better picture than this to sum it all up. Rangers are ecstatic with joy after scoring against Clydebank. But look at the despair written on the faces of the Bankies players, who felt they were about to create a sensation and beat the mighty men of Ibrox. That's football!

Scottish terracings, still the most critical, most knowledgeable, most enthusiastic of all.

I wrote in the introduction to the first *Scottish Football Book* all those years ago: 'As the writer of a daily football column, I never cease to marvel at the football erudition of the average club supporter, sometimes ruefully, I confess, because if I make a slip – and it may be the wrong name of a scorer in a match ten years past – a hundred indignant readers write to tell me of my mistake.

'No, there is not much you can tell the Scottish fan about football. He has made the game a lifelong study.

'I have been struck forcibly by the fact that football never changes. In the beginning of football, "a real guid gemme" was what the supporter relished most. He still does.'

And that still goes in this year of grace, 1979–80. Unfortunately, Scottish football is still on a crazy merry-go-round – or should it be up-and-down-go-round? We still seem to be reaching for the stars, then plunging to humiliating disaster. Look what happened in Argentina, for instance. A Scottish team we all felt was going to be great went to South America with the highest hopes – and failed miserably. But what's new? That's the story of our football lives.

Take this story from that first *Scottish Football Book:*

'In December 1954 Scotland had lost to the greatest team in the world, the fabulous Hungarians. But the courage and skill of the boys in blue had impressed the world. As the new year of 1955 dawned, our international hopes were high. It was felt that, at last, Scotland was moving with the times; that we had the foundations of a team to restore our tattered pride and that new ideas in training and trial matches could help us regain the British international championship.

Then came the match against England at Wembley on 2 April 1955, a golden spring day which, alack, will always be recalled as one of our blackest football chapters. For Scotland were trounced 7–2 and hopes that soon we would again be a force in world soccer fell to zero.

What went wrong? The selectors were blamed for not choosing Scotland's two outstanding players of the year, George Young of Rangers and Bobby Evans of Celtic. But what really happened was that Stanley Matthews was in the England team – and was superb. Scotland just couldn't tame him and so the match became a nightmare for Scotland and unlucky goalkeeper Fred Martin of Aberdeen.

And then . . . near triumph followed that Wembley gloom.

Scotland went on tour in the early summer of 1955 and became heroes. In three matches against the powerful opposition of Central Europe, Scotland were back on the map as a force in global football.

In results the record could have been more impressive. Scotland drew 2–2 with Yugoslavia, beat Austria 4–1 and lost to Hungary 3–1. But the results didn't matter. It was the way in which the Scots played which made the Continentals stop their sneering and admit that Britain was still the home of football.

Indeed, after the match in Budapest, hundreds of Hungarians waited outside their magnificent Nep stadium to acclaim a Scottish side which their officials described as "second only to Hungary in world football".

And we who were almost in tears at our team's inept display at Wembley could hardly believe our eyes as we cheered Scotland in Belgrade, Vienna and Budapest. For we saw Scotland playing real football again. Gordon Smith of Hibs, who became captain of the team when George Young was hurt in the opening game against Yugoslavia, summed it up: "We were a team of ball-workers, We concentrated on sheer football. We believed in ourselves.

Dundee United's Paul Hegarty, one of Scotland's 'finds', in action during his debut against Wales at Ninian Park

Opposite above: Scotland's Graeme Souness attacks in last season's home international against Wales, with Brian Flynn in opposition

Above: Argentinian wonder boy, Diego Maradona, moves clear of Scotland's Arthur Graham at Hampden

Opposite below: Liverpool midfield man Graeme Souness heads clear from England centre Bob Latchford during the game at Wembley

Left: Scotland centre half Gordon McQueen outjumps England defender Phil Thompson at Wembley

Below: One of Scotland's top defenders – David Narey of Dundee United

Left: What a header! It's a winner for Rangers and the scorer is centre half Colin Jackson in the League Cup Final against Aberdeen at Hampden

Opposite above left: Rangers' skipper Derek Johnstone heads clear from Hibs striker Bobby Hutchison in the Scottish Cup Final

Opposite above right: Another action shot from the Cup Final with Davie Cooper of Rangers moving clear of the Hibs defender

Opposite below left: Rangers' centre half Colin Jackson slides in desperately in a bid to stop Hibs' Ally McLeod

Opposite below right: Alex MacDonald, the midfield dynamo of Ibrox, sets up an attack in the Hampden Cup Final

Left: Celtic striker Tom McAdam in a duel with Brian Kinnear of Clyde

Opposite left: A mid-air duel in one of last season's Old Firm clashes between Alex MacDonald of Rangers and Jim Casey of Celtic

Opposite right: This battle is between Garry McDowall of Hamilton Acas and Bobby Russell of Morton

Opposite below: Aberdeen's flying winger Ian Scanlon bursts past Dundee United's veteran midfield man George Fleming

Below left: Hibernian's Arthur Duncan waits to tackle St Mirren's Billy Stark in a Premier League match

Below right: It's always a tough match, the Edinburgh derby! Here Ally McLeod of Hibs and Graham Shaw of Hearts battle for the ball

And every man-jack out there was playing his heart out." '

What better recipe is there for football success than that?

It was the recipe which helped Hearts to a 4–2 victory in the League Cup final against Motherwell in October, 1954. And that was no ordinary victory. It was a win which delighted every neutral in Scotland, sent Edinburgh fans delirious with joy and ended the most sorrowful story in Scottish football history.

For Hearts up till that October day had been the most mercurial team in Scotland. They could play brilliant football. They had produced wonderful teams. They had beaten the best. But it seemed that they invariably flopped at the critical time. And not for forty-eight years had Hearts won a major honour. In 1905–06 they beat Third Lanark in the final of the Scottish Cup at Ibrox. Since then – failure after failure.

But, after those forty-eight agonising years, Hearts came up trumps at Hampden and won with a fine display of football. And what a good Hearts team that was: Duff, Parker, McKenzie, Mackay, Glidden, Cumming, Souness, Conn, Bauld, Wardhaugh and Urquhart.

Motherwell are languishing these days. But in 1955 they had a star-studded side: Weir, Kilmarnock, McSeveney, Cox, Paton. Redpath, Hunter, Aitken, Bain, Humphries, Williams. So it was one of the epic League Cup finals, packed with excitement and clever football.

It was a year of triumph, too, for Aberdeen, who won the League championship for the first time, and for Clyde, who beat Celtic 1–0 in the Scottish Cup Final after a 1–1 draw.

Incidentally, it was in that first *Scottish Football Book* that Tommy McInally, the great Celtic inside forward, told the Europeans that the South Americans were going

Just a quarter of a century ago this young man made a dream debut for Rangers. His name – Alex Scott, destined to become one of the great wingers. And on 9 March 1955 he entranced the Rangers fans with a sparkling display in his first match. Alex scored a hat-trick against Falkirk (for whom he later played) and became the hero of Ibrox in his first game after leaving the Junior Bo'ness United. He went on to have a distinguished career with Rangers and Everton.

to be the great force in football. Tommy had first-hand experience of their football for he toured there with a Third Lanark select and he warned Scotland that the day of South American supremacy was about to dawn.

Now to the sad part of the first *Scottish Football Book*. One chapter was devoted to up-and-coming players. Who were they? They included Tommy Gemmell of St Mirren, Hugh Baird of Airdrie, John Davidson of Falkirk, George Brown of Clyde, John Harvey of Partick Thistle, Ian Rae of Falkirk, Alistair MacLeod of Third Lanark and Jimmy Miller of Rangers. Only Ally

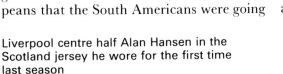

Liverpool centre half Alan Hansen in the Scotland jersey he wore for the first time last season

Many famous players have swept across the soccer scene in the past twenty-five years, but few have been more accomplished than Ian MacMillan, that great inside forward who found fame with Airdrie and Rangers.

MacLeod is still to the fore in the game. And it's sad to think how many great players slip out of football.

Take the team who played at Wembley in 1955: Martin (Aberdeen), Cunningham (Preston), Haddock (Clyde), Docherty (Preston), Davidson (Partick Thistle), Cumming (Hearts), McKenzie (Partick Thistle), Johnstone (Manchester City), Reilly (Hibernian), MacMillan (Airdrie), Ring (Clyde).

Only Tommy Docherty is still playing a part in big-time football as a manager. It seems a pity that the great ability and love of football these players had is now lost to the game.

Nevertheless, there may have been tragedy in the past twenty-five years of Scottish football, but there were magic moments, too. Let's hope there's as much excitement, as much glamour in the next quarter of a century.

DOUG'S DAY OF DISASTER

No Aberdeen player looked forward more eagerly to the League Cup final than centre half Doug Rougvie. For he had waited a long, long time to make his first appearance at Hampden – seven years precisely.

Patience, however, had always been a virtue with the big man from Fife. It was away back in 1972 that Jimmy Bonthrone, then Aberdeen manager, spotted Doug. But if he thought he had stepped into the big-time at Pittodrie, Rougvie was quickly dis-illusioned. He looked the part alright, tall, strong, commanding. He played well in the reserves. But he was too versatile for he was equally at home in defence, midfield and attack and it seemed he would never estab-lish himself.

For years it was the same story, although Aberdeen managers came and went – Bon-throne, Ally MacLeod, Billy McNeill – the big defender could count on the fingers of one hand his number of first team matches.

Most people would have become dis-heartened. He was a good player and he knew it and many would have been demanding transfers. Not Rougvie. His enthusiasm never waned, he was as ambi-tious as ever and in season 1978-79 it all paid off.

Under new manager Alex Ferguson, Rougvie came into the Aberdeen team wearing the number four shirt against Hamilton Acas in a League Cup-tie. Alas, he dropped out again. Then he took over, for three games, at right back. Again he vanished from the first eleven scene.

But in November Doug Rougvie made it at last, at centre half, his favourite position but a role in which at the start of the season he had appeared no better choice than third behind Willie Garner and Alex McLeish.

With both out injured, Doug got his big chance and seized it so well that Garner and McLeish, fit again, couldn't shake him. Before the League Cup final on Saturday, 31 March 1979, he had played eighteen matches in a row, seemed to be improving in every one – and couldn't wait to play in his first cup final at Hampden....

For manager Alex Ferguson it was also a first cup final as a club boss. But he felt his first job was to make sure his players didn't 'freeze' as they had done in the Scot-tish Cup Final the year before, also against Rangers, and fail to play to form.

'The lads know they are good enough to win,' he said.

That, though, was also the theme of Rangers manager John Greig, who had to sit helpless and hope his old colleagues and present employees would take the League Cup away from Hampden bedecked in the Ibrox blue. Hoping to collect his first major piece of silverware since he moved upstairs from the dressing-room to the managerial office, he was nervous but said: 'This is a great team. I feel we will win.'

And Rangers, as usual, started the book-makers' favourites, but few felt the thirty-fourth League Cup final would be a repeat of the first when Rangers demolished Aber-deen 4-0.

Poor Doug Rougvie! What should have been his day of triumph turned to disaster when he was ordered off in the League Cup final against Rangers

One of Scotland's most reliable defenders is Aberdeen's Chic McLelland

It was a sunshine final. After the bleak winter and the deep freeze which had practically shut down Scottish football for months, a crowd of 54,000 welcomed the bright afternoon, and looked ahead to a fascinating match.

At the start no player was in better form than Doug Rougvie. He was magnificent in the heart of the Dons defence, winning every ball in the air and giving his colleagues inspiration. It was, however, anything but sunshine soccer in the first half, with Rangers on top but hardly at their best – a quiet, scrappy 45 minutes.

How different in the second session. For the League Cup final became the most controversial and incident-packed of them all – full of drama, suspense and argument.

The final came to life in the fifty-ninth minute. That's when Aberdeen scored, and big Doug Rougvie felt he would at last win a cup final victory badge. It wasn't the most magnificent of goals, but it looked as though it would be the vital one. The build-up was something special, a move right out of the Pittodrie manual of football wizardry.

Joe Harper and Gordon Strachan began it with a fine one-two. When the ball finally came across goal, however, Sandy Jardine or Peter McCloy might have knocked it away. But they didn't, and Duncan Davidson couldn't believe his luck as he saw

the ball flying directly to his forehead. He was so surprised that his header was weak. Thankfully goalkeeper McCloy flopped down on the ball, seemed to have it safely in his hands, then allowed it to slip out and bounce over the line.

And McLelland's full back partner Stuart Kennedy is also a fine Scotland player

If that was a fluke, so was Rangers' equaliser in the seventy-seventh minute.

Rangers hit back hard. They always do.

But the equaliser was a disaster for Aberdeen. Goalkeeper Bobby Clark had injured an arm but referee Ian Foote didn't stop play so that the player could have attention. Then, from outside the penalty box, Alex MacDonald shot. Despite his injury, Clark had the shot covered all the way – until it struck John McMaster on the shin and skited into the net well away from the despairing Clark.

And then came the moment of tragedy for big Doug Rougvie. Only eight minutes remained. The final seemed certain to go into extra time. But with the ball yards away there was a clash between Rougvie and Derek Johnstone, the Rangers captain who had been moved up front in a bid to find more zip in the attack.

Johnstone was on the ground, Rougvie was staring at him in amazement. And then he was almost in tears as the referee came haring down the field, and sent him off.

Rougvie, who had been previously booked for a foul on Davie Cooper, couldn't believe it. He protested that he hadn't touched Johnstone. But the referee thought differently and so poor Doug Rougvie became only the second player in Scottish history to be sent off in a final, following in the footsteps of Jock Buchanan of Rangers, who was sent for an early bath in the 1929 Scottish Cup Final when Kilmarnock won 2-0.

Arguments raged long afterwards. Did Johnstone fall, or was he pushed? No one will ever really know, and few indeed saw the incident.

Poor Rougvie. His great day had ended in disaster but his consolation was that Scottish League officials decided there was nothing in the rule-book that prevented him receiving his runners-up medal. Yes, runners-up. For, with Rougvie off, Rangers scored a sensational winner in injury-time.

Big Doug was really in tears when he saw it. For he was convinced that if he had still been on the field it would have been pre-

One of Scotland's up-and-coming midfield maestros is John McMaster of Aberdeen

vented. Still, it was a splendid goal, fit to win any final, and it came when Rangers centre half, the veteran Colin Jackson, rose up to head an accurate free-kick taken by Tommy McLean powerfully past the helpless Bobby Clark in the third minute of extra time.

And so Aberdeen's dream of glory faded once again. Perhaps Rangers just deserved to win, but tears had to be shed for the Dons, who finished with ten men and an injured goalkeeper. And most felt that the penalty suffered by Rougvie was far too severe.

Still, it had been a niggly game, with referee Foote, apart from booking Rougvie

The outstanding sweeper in Scotland – that's how Aberdeen fans describe their captain, Willie Miller

Happy Dons. But that was before the League Cup final. Joe Harper and Drew Jarvie lead the fun at pre-final training

and then sending him off, taking the names of Drew Jarvie, Gordon Strachan and Joe Harper of Aberdeen and Tommy McLean and Alex Miller of Rangers.

One big question remained. What happens to Aberdeen when they reach Hampden? Once again they failed to play as they can play. For too much of the game they appeared to lack confidence.

It was a pity, of course, that both teams were without key players who were injured – Tom Forsyth of Rangers and Dom Sullivan of Aberdeen and perhaps the Dons were harder hit as the smooth raiding and clever generalship of Sullivan plays a big part in their plans.

The teams were:

Rangers: McCloy, Jardine, Dawson, Johnstone, Jackson, MacDonald, McLean, Russell, Urquhart, Smith, Cooper.
Subs: Miller, Parlane.
Aberdeen: Clark, Kennedy, McLelland, McMaster, Rougvie, Miller, Strachan, Archibald, Harper, Jarvie, Davidson.

Subs: McLeish, Cooper.
Referee: Ian Foote (Glasgow).

This was the way to Hampden for the finalists:

Rangers
First round – Rangers 3, Albion Rovers 0; Albion Rovers 0, Rangers 1
Second round – Rangers 3, Forfar Athletic 0; Forfar 1, Rangers 4
Third round – Rangers 3, St Mirren 2; St Mirren 0, Rangers 0
Quarter final – Rangers 1, Arbroath 0; Arbroath 1, Rangers 2
Semi-final – Rangers 3, Celtic 2 (Hampden after extra time)

Aberdeen
First round – bye
Second round – Meadowbank Thistle 0, Aberdeen 4; Aberdeen 5, Meadowbank 0
Third round – Hamilton Acas 0, Aberdeen 1; Aberdeen 7, Hamilton 1
Quarter final – Ayr United 3, Aberdeen 3; Aberdeen 3, Ayr 0
Semi-final – Hibs 0, Aberdeen 1 (Dens Park after extra time)

SO NEAR TO GLORY...then Rangers' European Cup Dream fades

In the end, Rangers failed. Their dreams of becoming European Cup champions at last, faded on their own Ibrox on a dull March night. Nevertheless, Rangers showed that they have grown up in Europe – that they have players to match the best on the Continent – that they have a style to rival that of anyone in the world of modern soccer.

It was in the neat Dutch town of Eindhoven on the night of 1 November 1978 that Rangers came of age in the European Cup, and gained perhaps the greatest victory of all in their long, illustrious history.

It followed a fine win over Juventus, who were beaten 2–0 at Ibrox on 27 September 1978, after Rangers had displayed flair and a new technique in losing only 1–0 to the Italians in Turin on 13 September.

And it gave Scotland hope that Rangers could become the second Scottish side, after Celtic's immortal Lisbon Lions, to win the premier and most torrid tournament of all, the European Cup.

It was an epic victory.

Rangers demanded heroics from a thin blue line in their bid for European glory on the night of the second leg of the European Cup-tie against PSV Eindhoven, who were among the hot favourites for the trophy and tipped to win the second leg easily after holding the Scottish champions to a 0–0 draw at Ibrox on 18 October.

Rangers' defence had been sadly depleted. They were without centre half Colin Jackson, suffering from a groin injury. They had to field Tom Forsyth who wasn't fully fit and key man Tom McLean was also hurt. But McLean had to play, for manager John Greig, whose tactics against Juventus had been the talk of Europe, felt the wee winger was his most important player.

Rangers' new boss believed McLean's sagacity, his cleverness in setting up chances from the most unexpected positions and his ability to bewilder defences with accurate passes and crosses were Rangers' main hope of getting a goal which would be among the most vital the Ibrox team had ever scored.

And so it proved.

This is my report from Holland, one of the happiest I have ever sent in a long career in football journalism, for it concerned one of the outstanding victories any Scottish side has ever achieved. The date-line is Eindhoven. The date is 1 November 1978.

'Rangers flowed fluently into the top rankings in Europe here with a display of fascinating football that dimmed the lights of PSV Eindhoven, among the favourites for the European Cup.

It was Rangers' greatest victory in Europe – perhaps the best in their long history. For not only did the Scottish champions, given little chance of winning here by even their most fervent supporters, play modern, glittering soccer that was as stylish as Real Madrid's, but they also showed remarkable courage.

So near and yet so far. Cologne goalkeeper Harald Schumacher foils Rangers as they try so desperately to score a vital goal in the European Cup tie at Ibrox

The 3-2 victory which puts them into the quarter final of the European Cup rocked the Continent. No wonder. This was the first time Eindhoven had lost at home in any European match – and they've played twenty-seven.

The shaken Dutch fans couldn't believe it, couldn't realize their heroes of total football were being bewildered by a Scottish side who never stopped trying to turn on sweet, scientific soccer, who never lost their heads even in the face of a late furious Dutch assault.

And yet Rangers lost a goal in only 30 seconds – and were behind again a few

minutes after a glorious equaliser. They took the field with two players, Tom Forsyth and Tommy McLean, less than one hundred per cent fit and with goalkeeper Peter McCloy the victim of a late stomach bug.

But in the end they had their overjoyed fans leaping with delight as the disconsolate Dutch followers departed hurriedly before the end.

No praise is too high for Rangers. They are fast becoming masters of the European scene. Gone are the days of the big blooter, the big kick, the cavalry charges. Now it's the delicate flick, the tender touch, the astute use of the open space.

The goal they scored to win an astonishing 3-2 victory will go down in history. It was 2-2 with Eindhoven desperately attacking to get the goal which would take them

through. The tension for the Scots in the 29,000 crowd was unbearable.

But not for those cute little Rangers, Bobby Russell and Tommy McLean.

A break found the Eindhoven defence anything but total. McLean held the ball,

And it's the cool Schumacher again who grabs the ball from the onrushing Tom Forsyth of Rangers

looked up, saw Russell haring into the open space, dispatched a cunning pass – and howled with glee as Robert the audacious tricked outcoming goalkeeper Tony van Engelen with the coolness of a European veteran to give Rangers their wonderful win.

Rangers won't score a better goal this season – perhaps this century. Yes, it was as good as that – a gem, a masterpiece, a football confection to be wrapped in blue ribbons. Cool, clever, delicately honed and ruthlessly finished.

Yet less than a minute from the start anyone putting a bet on Rangers to win would have been considered headbanger No. 1. For only 30 seconds had passed when Rangers lost a goal.

It was a prime example of the wonderful football the Dutch play so well. Foolishly, Rangers gave the ball away. And in a lightning raid the sorry boys in blue didn't realize what had happened until Harry Lubse had flashed a swift cross from Willy Jensen past the startled and helpless McCloy.

After that, it became an extraordinary contest. Rangers played all the football. Eindhoven were content to contain them, to laze around. But at times Rangers' build-up seemed too slow, too laborious. And even though they made several chances it looked as though they were out. It was all rather unreal, hardly exciting, certainly not an epic European cup-tie.

But Rangers were playing the right game. They were patient, happy to set up delightful moves, confident their neat football would pay off in the end.

It did and if the first half was as serene as a Dutch windmill in a mild breeze the second had every Scot biting his nails with anxiety – and cheering Rangers to the echo.

Once again it was Rangers who provided the skilful touches, the fine raids. And they seized a dramatic equaliser when Alex MacDonald surprised the tall Dutch defenders by getting first to one of those accurate crosses from McLean.

But gloom soon chased Scottish smiles. Just as they had done to Scotland in Mendoza, the Dutch hit back inside three minutes when Gerry Deijkers swooped on the ball as Rangers' defenders hesitated, and drove it into the net.

That was when Rangers earned their blue badges of courage. They lost neither head nor heart, continued to play their new football and got the equaliser which was enough to see them through.

Kenny Watson smashed in a vicious shot in Holland's own total football manner, Derek Johnstone got a touch – and it was 2-2.

By this time, of course, Eindhoven had shrugged off their lethargy and their almost contemptuous indifference to a game they appeared to think they could win at a stroll.

Now it was the Rangers rearguard who were the heroes, stemming the red tidal wave, sometimes desperately but always effectively.

And then came that Russell goal which made the score 3-2 and completed what will go down in history as a Scottish dream result – a result obtained by traditional Scottish resilience, new patience and magnificent skills.

Let's not carp at Rangers now. Critics are suggesting already that Juventus and Eindhoven were perhaps not as good as they were believed to be.

Nonsense! The truth is that they played only as Rangers allowed them to – for now Rangers are among the giants, a team of style and distinction, a match for the best.

Manager John Greig's faith in his system and his team paid off. He took calculated risks with McCloy, Forsyth and McLean. But how that worked.

Cologne star Heinz Flohe, whose marvellous skills entranced the Ibrox crowd in the European Cup

The real Ibrox winner. Hennes Weisweiller of Cologne had too many tricks up his sleeve for Rangers in the European Cup

'Look out, Europe, we're really coming over now – that's the message from Ibrox.'

So it was praise all the way for Rangers. On the Continent they read with awe about the sensational victory. And Eindhoven manager Cees Rijvers, forlorn and distressed after his unexpected defeat was nevertheless full of praise for Rangers. 'They surprised us,' he said, 'because they played imaginative and stylish football, the likes of which I didn't expect from a British side. They are a truly fine side and must have a splendid chance of winning the European Cup which I thought we were going to win this year.'

But John Greig was cautious. 'There's a long way to go and a lot to do yet,' he said. He was right.

For the quarter final against Cologne, the West German champions, on 6 March 1979, Rangers lost much of their zip, some of their style. Indeed, in the beautiful stadium under the shadow of the magnificent Cologne cathedral on the banks of the Rhine, Rangers lived as dangerously as they ever have in Europe, had more escapes than Colditz – but returned a result that had their thousands of travelling fans hailing them as heroes.

The 1-0 defeat by Cologne in the first leg was a near epic, with John Greig's tactics keeping the eager Germans at bay, although this type of soccer wasn't a tonic for the true blues. More times than the Scots cared to imagine Rangers tottered on the brink of the precipice. At least five times the warriors in the redoubtable Ibrox defence cleared on the goal-line. Peter McCloy made saves that bordered on the miraculous. And Cologne kicked themselves for failing to take advantage of half a dozen golden opportunities.

Yet Rangers take praise for sticking to their herculean task with the determination and gallantry of the Light Brigade, although this was no thin red line set up in the impressive Mungersdorf Stadium – but a solid, thick blue line it was!

The aim was to absorb the exacting assaults of Cologne, who felt that only a victory by at least three goals would give them hope of winning the quarter final.

How well Rangers coped. For it was a battle of tired troops, an army sadly affected by casualties.

Yet the Rangers side, with players from the reserves such as Jim Denny and Billy Urquhart and with several regulars such as Tom Forsyth, Tom McLean and Alex MacDonald anything but one hundred per cent fit, kept their heads, stuck to the roles manager John Greig had allotted them and almost got the draw they wanted.

It's true that Rangers didn't perfect the Continental defensive tactics as well as they

had against Juventus and Eindhoven. They played it much deeper, allowing Cologne to stride forward venomously but yet stopping World Cup star Heinz Flohe and company from getting the goals they so desperately needed. It's also true that luck was with the Scots and against the Germans.

Rangers had skipper Sandy Jardine marking Flohe so tightly that this fine player must have been gagging at the whiffs of Sandy's embrocation. Only once did Flohe escape Jardine and that was fatal for Rangers. For Flohe at last crossed the ball he wanted and from that Dieter Muller scored the only goal of the match. It was hardly a classic for the ball bobbed around agonizingly in McCloy's goal area before it was nodded sneakily into the net by the Cologne striker.

In the end, everyone felt it was a good result for the scratch Rangers side on the cold, windy night on the foreign field of the Mungersdorf Stadium.

Alas, it wasn't.

It was the prelude to the shattering of Rangers' dream.

It was a strange, sad, silent night at Ibrox on Thursday, 22 March 1979, as the dream was shattered, as Rangers' chance of European immortality slipped quietly away from them.

The match had been postponed from the scheduled Wednesday date because bad weather which had effected Scottish football so disastrously, mischievously returned and Rangers had to mount a massive snow-clearing operation before the second leg could go on the following night.

Time after time we had seen Rangers quit the European scene in a blaze of hectic activity, of blood and thunder assaults which were calmly rebuffed by mature, responsible and immoveable Continental defenders, of crackling firework displays which had their fans bellowing – and opposing rearguards laughing.

Rangers are all smiles before leaving Largs
for their European Cup tie with Cologne. But
they weren't so happy after losing at Ibrox

It was all so different this time when
Rangers, by drawing 1-1 with Cologne following their 0-1 defeat in Germany, failed
to find their way into the European Cup
semi-finals.

Rangers played with the patience
demanded by their manager, kept their
heads, tried to play intelligent soccer, seldom resorted to the mighty lunge, high
cross and despairing header.

What went wrong then?

Even when Tommy McLean scored a

bright and cheeky goal from a free kick
three minutes from the end to salvage Ibrox
pride and make it a 1-1 draw instead of
humiliating defeat, why were so many of
the 44,000 fans on their way home and the
stadium a valley of brooding silence?

My view was that Rangers fell between
two stools, the widely varying tactics which
are still argued about by the expert coaches
– the red-hot urgency which so many still
believe should be the aim of home teams in
the premier tournament and the calculat-
ing, cunning, contrived cat-and-mouse
game beloved of the Italians.

Did Greig, whose tactics were impeccable
in the matches which saw Rangers become
lions in Europe with the defeats of Juventus

and Eindhoven, plan it the right way in the crucial match?

He was right to ask his players not to panic, to play controlled football, to be patient.

But too many Rangers fell into a too-slow, too-dull method. Perhaps if the game had been played, as it should have been, the night before, it might have been different. Perhaps Rangers lost some of their zest, for they had reached their peak presumably on the Wednesday. But that went for Cologne, too.

Anyhow, not until it was too late, not until after Dieter Muller had in 47 minutes scored the goal which sounded Rangers' European Cup death-knell, did the Scots realize they needed much more urgency to try to upset the tight Cologne defence, to get their home crowd right behind them.

The truth is that, on the night, Rangers just weren't good enough and fell to a better team. But what a pity Rangers failed at the vital time to find the form, the belief in themselves, the sophistication and application which shattered Juventus and Eindhoven.

As that wily old fox, Cologne manager Hennes Weisweiller, said: 'Rangers did not play as well as they did against us in Cologne. They lacked a system and after 15 minutes we all knew we would reach the semi-finals.'

Greig, so honest, so gallant in his most heart-breaking experience since he took over as Ibrox manager, refused to make excuses or blame his players who, he said, gave Rangers all anyone could give.

'But,' he said, 'on the night we were just not good enough.'

And that's the whole story. Perhaps Rangers were outfoxed by Weisweiller, although Greig made it clear Cologne played exactly as he thought they would, with the team he was convinced they would field.

But the splendid Herbert Zimmerman, who attacked with spirit and panache in Cologne, was given a different role which he performed equally effectively. He marked the menacing Gordon Smith out of the game.

Nevertheless, Rangers had chances and even if one had been taken early on it might have been so different. But when Muller scored it was all over. Rangers then needed three goals to win.

Cologne were the best team Rangers met in the European Cup, deft in attack, commanding in midfield, flexible in defence. They also had players more skilled than Rangers. They were pretty good actors, too, and if the injuries they said they had sustained had been real Weisweiller would have been handing out at least half a dozen iron crosses for bravery in continuing on the pitch.

In the end, Rangers were beaten but not disgraced. They had injury worries and, perhaps, if they had been at full strength they might have made the semi-finals. But I doubt that.

Yet they put up a magnificent show in Europe and brought back pride to Scotland. If the flair wasn't there, if pride and passion and ecstasy gave way to agony at Ibrox, there were for Rangers fans entrancing memories of wonderful European moments.

And, who knows, Rangers might do even better in Europe this season....

WHEN THE ACTION'S HOT...

... football becomes the most exciting game in the world. Pulses pound. Frayed vocal chords make voices hoarse. Electricity hums in the air.

What a keeper! Billy Thomson of St Mirren makes a splendid save in a game against Rangers

Yes, when the drama unfolds, when players put their hearts into it, football becomes a theatre.

And here, in these pictures which capture all the thrills, the tension, the emotion, the spills, the rancour of our great game, you relive the acts of the season ...

Unorthodox, not according to the book – but
fine goalkeeping nevertheless, as Hugh
Sproat of Ayr United dashes out to clear
from Bobby Graham of Hamilton Acas

Hey, steady on fellows, keep the head!
That's the plea from Hearts goalkeeper
Thomson Allan as Tommy McLean of
Rangers and Jim Jefferies of Hearts fail to
see eye to eye

Oh, my aching head! And Derek Parlane of
Rangers doesn't look too happy as Jim
Leighton goes up to clear his Aberdeen
goal-line

Still going strong during the season was the
last of the Lisbon Lions, Bobby Lennox of
Celtic

Just a couple of song and dance men? No,
the stalwarts keeping time here are Drew
Busby of Hearts and Joe Wark of
Motherwell

Suspense! Who'll get to the ball first – Tom
Forsyth of Rangers or Harald Schumacher,
the Cologne keeper? The German won and
Cologne went on to beat Rangers in the
European Cup

No way through! Goal-grabber John Bourke
of Kilmarnock is baulked this time by St
Johnstone defenders

Anxiety is written over the face of St Mirren
striker Frank McGarvey as he waits for the
result of a shot against Clydebank

Acrobatics as Bobby Reid, the unlucky St
Mirren centre half who missed most of the
season because of injuries, flies through the
air and over Sandy Frame of Partick Thistle

Flat out – that's Lawrie Williams, Dumbarton
keeper

Stern action in a Rangers triumph. An Alex
MacDonald effort flies goalwards as the
Scots beat Juventus in the European Cup

THE DEFEAT THAT CHANGED MY LIFE
by Paul Hegarty of Dundee United
Scotland's Players' Player of the Year

No player enjoys being knocked out of the Scottish Cup – particularly by a team from a lower division – but I have never lived to regret the day we lost to St Mirren at Love Street in 1977.

The Paisley side, in the first division then, adapted much better than ourselves to the icey conditions and came back after losing an early goal to beat us by 4–1. As we trooped off Love Street dejectedly that afternoon, I felt as sick about the result as the rest of my United team-mates. I didn't know it at the time but that defeat was the most significant game of my career.

For, instead of playing in the next round of the Cup three weeks later, United arranged a friendly match against Everton at Goodison Park. And it was that game against the English First Division side that changed me from a struggling striker into a successful centre half.

I suppose a couple of things had been against me when I signed for United from Hamilton in November, 1974. First of all, it took me several months to adjust from part-time to full-time training. And, believe me, full-time training doesn't come any tougher than it does at Tannadice.

Secondly, I was asked to take over the hardest job in Scottish football . . . replacing Andy Gray in the Dundee United attack. He was probably the best forward United had ever had on their books and he was a player I admired tremendously, both to watch and to play alongside, as we did for a spell before he moved to Aston Villa.

I tried hard to be another Andy Gray but I knew within myself that I wasn't sharp enough ever to be that good. United manager Jim McLean obviously appreciated the problem, too. For in that match against Everton he decided to try me in the middle of the defence.

In fact, I had played there before for a spell against Celtic in a League game at Parkhead when Alex Rennie had been hurt. But the Everton game was my first full ninety minutes as a central defender and, before the game, I believed it would be a daunting task.

Everton were fielding Bob Latchford at centre forward and I knew that I would be up against a player who had, at one time, been the most expensive in Britain following his £350,000 move from Birmingham City.

However, I played well in a goalless draw, although I must say that game didn't altogether convince me that my true position was centre half.

There were still doubts in my mind because, after all, the game had been a meaningless friendly and perhaps Latchford hadn't exactly tried too hard to give me a rough time.

The boss, however, obviously considered that I had done all he wanted . . . and since then I have been the regular centre half in the United line-up.

For me, playing centre half requires four essentials – ability in the air; ability to read the game so that you can try to cut off the

Paul Hegarty – the players' choice as Player of the Year

supply of the ball to the forward players from midfield; a knowledge and feel for when to commit yourself in the tackle; and, more and more in the modern game, an ability to use the ball out of defence.

I consider myself to have a fair amount of natural skill in the first three areas and I know within myself that I have to work hard to keep my passing up to scratch.

But there is plenty of encouragement to work hard at Tannadice. I have never known anyone so dedicated to the game as our boss and his willingness to work at the game rubs off on everyone at the club.

As I have said already, it took me several months to make the successful transition from being a part-time player to a full-time one and I don't know of any other club where players work harder in training.

But that is only part of the way the manager has brought so much success to the club. He always has an exact knowledge of opponents and that obviously is a tremendous aid now that the game is so tight in Scotland.

Last season, when I finally convinced myself that centre half was my true position, was full of career highlights that I shall never forget no matter how far I might go in the game or how long I might stay in it.

Obviously, I enjoyed being part of a team pushing for the League championship for so long. There was a great atmosphere in the dressing-room – not tension but excitement. It was terrific to be part of that.

And away from the Premier League there was also plenty to get excited about. I shall, for instance, always remember leading the team out for the UEFA Cup game against Standard Liege in Ghent.

It was the first time I had captained the side in Europe and it was an atmosphere completely new to me. There was something really special about following a piper out on to a pitch on the continent knowing that I was there to represent Scotland in some way.

In fact, although Dundee United have lost money at times by playing in Europe, I know that the manager and all the players enjoy the change of scene and change of opposition. It becomes very difficult playing so many matches full of tension in the Premier League and I believe that Europe makes a very pleasant change.

Of course, we didn't manage to get past the first round against Standard but I believe Rangers did so well in the European Cup, beating Juventus and PSV Eindhoven before going out to Cologne, simply because they were able to enjoy the change in conditions and atmosphere which Europe provides.

But back to my own highlights. The next one I would like to mention is my selection for the full Scotland pool for the first time. Having been chosen for the squad, I felt very much like a new boy when I reported with the rest of the players but my lasting impression was how welcome manager Jock Stein immediately made me feel. And what a thrill to play at Wembley, even though we lost to England.

In no time Stein made me relax and it seemed I had been one of the lads for a long time. I think, in fact, it is that kind of Stein magic that will help the national side go places in the future. And, clearly, I would like to be part of that future.

I have intentionally left the biggest moment of the season to the end simply because it is the memory I shall cherish most. That was the night in the Albany Hotel in Glasgow when I was named as Scotland's Players' Player of the Year.

At times you think you are a good player and you can't help listening to people in the game and outside of it expressing the view that you are contributing something to football. But to actually be presented with an award from the other players in the game means that you can finally believe you aren't a bad player!

Not that I am getting big headed. I know I can still learn a lot about the game and, hopefully, become a far better player as my career progresses. But that award from my fellow-professionals meant the world to me.

THE LONGEST TIE...
it went off and off and off

They billed it as the most famous Scottish cup-tie never played. For it took twenty-nine inspections of Kingsmills Park and a forty-nine-day delay to put the second round game between Inverness Thistle and Falkirk into the folklore of Scottish football.

It ended on Thursday, 22 February 1979, when the fishermen, firemen, clerks and outfitters of Thistle and the professionals of Falkirk burst impatiently onto a pitch that was yellow and grey and green and scarred – but at last playable.

The tie should have been played on 6 January but because of the severe winter weather it had been postponed.

And once again it was Scotland for records. For in this little country we have seen the biggest British crowds, the biggest scores, the clubs like Celtic and Rangers who win so many games. After all, no team is likely to score more goals in the cup than Arbroath who sent Aberdeen Bon Accord crashing to a 36-0 defeat last century and just pipped Dundee Harp who beat another luckless Aberdeen side, the Rovers, by 35-0 that same day of 1885.

But this match won't go down in the book of Mr Guinness. It wasn't really the longest tie, a misfortune which belongs to the 1963 tie between Airdrie and Stranraer, postponed thirty-three times.

It caused a sensation, however, even in Fleet Street, which sent one of its most distinguished representatives to report the match when it was eventually played, who caught the atmosphere of the game perfectly.

He wrote: 'On a bright icy afternoon in that corner of the country where the Arctic weather comes to test itself before spreading across Britain there were some nice moments to cherish.

'The zealot pacing a lonely corner with a placard declaring, "The End is Nigh" was not for once ignored. "Never mind the end, Jimmy...are we even getting started?" called one supporter.

'The best joke of the day was when the players came out. "Is that ye, Lofty? Hell, you've changed." Fair comment probably as Thistle fans hadn't seen their team perform since before Christmas.'

One oddity of the longest tie of the season was that as the referee is paid £2.50 for each time he calls off a game, Mr Alastair Kidd's postponement perks meant that he had earned more from not allowing the game to be played than the entire Inverness forward line who finally did take part. How's that for a tricky question in soccer quizzes of the future?

Alas for Thistle who, because of the weather had to kick off an hour earlier than most of us sit down to lunch, and whose tiny stand was only half full even at 20p a backside. The tie as a contest was over before the coffee was being served in the posh Inverness hotels.

Poor Thistle! They lost, according to Ian Archer in the *Scottish Daily Express*, because they incurred the wrath of the Lord. Said Ian: 'Falkirk and a stern Highland minister who believes that even the Free Presbyterian Church is a dangerous bunch of misty-eyed radicals combined to beat Thistle.

'A multitude of 1,543 watched a muddy game and paid some £784.10 to be able to say, "I was there – eventually," and they put their souls at risk because 74-year-old Ewan McQueen, a long-time supporter who lives a corner kick away from the park, had objected. The Minister, so incensed that the club were breaking the Sunday peace by lighting bonfires on the pitch, had shouted over the fence and predicted disaster.

Meet some of the men they applaud at Brockville. The Falkirk personalities include:

'And so – as all students of comparative theology will be glad to know – it turned out.

'And Thistle were left to count the fringe benefits – a sell-out of the second edition of the programme and, at last, space in the big newspapers.'

Whether or not divine guidance had anything to do with it, the match was over after 20 minutes. That was when the Inverness fans who had pleaded for the tie to go on spent the rest of the afternoon trying to persuade referee Brian McGinlay to stop it.

And the man who led these pleas was Thistle goalkeeper John Rae, who must have wished the tie had been postponed until at least the end of his playing career.

The sad truth was that the Second Division aces were far too good for the men of

Goalkeeper Bobby McKell

Manager Billy Little

Midfield man Paul Leetion

Forward Alastair McRoberts

the Highland League, although it might have been different if Thistle's top scorer, Jim Guyan, hadn't missed an early chance.

Falkirk took the lead in 12 minutes with an Ally McRoberts header and added to it with goals from Brian Brown and Joe McCallan within a six-minute spell. When winger John Perry added the fourth it was all over and the fans drifted away into the early mid-afternoon gloom.

Thistle had lost and the gate receipts hardly compensated Inverness for the cost of snow-clearing over the long days.

But no one will ever forget this tie. Programmes for the first unplayed match have become collector's items. Fans who trekked in from remote areas became folk heroes, counting their scores by the number of false starts they have endured. And the fans will remember the late sturdy rally by Thistle and a few mazy dribbles by Skye lobster fisherman Jimmy Inglis.

It was indeed a saga, though I doubt if any piper will be writing or playing a lament for that frozen winter.

MORTON'S MAN OF MAGIC – Andy Ritchie, Player of the Year

Just over two years ago, Andy Ritchie left Celtic Park for Morton as makeweight in a transfer deal. This season he became Scotland's Player of the Year. And he won the most prestigious award in the game – awarded by the Scottish Football Writers' Association – in a season in which more candidates than ever were in with a shout, including the elegant Paul Hegarty of Dundee United, who was the players' union's choice, Willie Miller of Aberdeen, Sandy Jardine of Rangers, Alan Rough of Partick Thistle and Bobby Clark of Aberdeen.

Andy Ritchie is a character, a personality. His style is languid. Opposing managers have said they wouldn't have him in their sides – but they shake with apprehension every time he gains possession of the ball.

His outrageous gifts border on genius. His close control rivals that of Kenny Dalglish. He hits a dead ball harder than Peter Lorimer.

As a colleague says, he doesn't merely make the ball talk – he gets it to give speeches. He has earned success by doing his own unorthodox thing which the fans love.

Some of the goals he has scored would have been envied by Pele. For Andy Ritchie has a Pandora's box of Latin and Continental tricks, bending and curving shots so easily. A high percentage of these are struck from long distances, a few from dead ball situations, many are fancifully curved.

How does he achieve it? Is it a special gift? Here is Andy talking about his banana benders which are the goalkeeper's nightmare:

'In 1974 I motored to West Germany to support Scotland in the World Cup and one day I wandered into Brazil's training camp. There I saw the great Rivelino bending the ball round eight men in the defensive wall.

'I thought I'd like to have a go at it and I discovered I had the same facility with my right foot. Mind you, I can't bend the ball round eight men but I notice that defences are increasing their walls from four men to six when I take free kicks so I suppose that's a back-handed compliment to me.

'While my shots don't bend as much as Rivelino's, I think I have my own trademark. They bend and then dip just to give an extra twist.

'It's really all about weighting the ball properly. Don't ask me how it's done. A gift, I suspect. You can either do it or you can't.'

Now Andy is the toast of Greenock, the idol of the kids.

But it wasn't always easy for the big fellow. Indeed, it was his father who forced him into football. Grins Andy: 'The turning point in my life came when I was fifteen. I lived in Bellshill and it was raining and I was sitting on the settee at home, wishing the rain would stop and thinking about an apprenticeship as a fitter.

'Football was just a hobby then and I had never thought about playing it profes-

Andy Ritchie receives his Player of the Year award from Hugh Taylor, President of the Scottish Football Writers' Association

sionally. Then the manager of Bellshill YMCA, whom I'd had some games for, came to the door to tell me Middlesbrough were holding trials at Cumbernauld United's ground that afternoon.

'He wanted me to go as he didn't think many lads would turn up in that weather. I remember saying: "I'm not going out to play in the rain," when my dad told me immediately I was going whether I liked it or not. We had a right old argument but he won and I went, reluctantly.

'But it was incredible what happened. I played in midfield then, did well and scored

Andy Ritchie, Scotland's Player of the Year, goes into typical action

a goal. After that game, Stan Anderson, who was then manager of Middlesbrough, offered to sign me as a professional even though it was only an apprenticeship.

'The place was crawling with scouts and before I went home I had invitations to train with Rangers, Celtic and Manchester United. I couldn't believe it.

'And it was thanks to my dad, who made me get out and play that wet day.'

Scotland won as far as Andy was concerned and after a spell with Kirkintilloch Rob Roy he settled in with Celtic. But Parkhead was then crawling with celebrities. So it was no happy-ever-after story for Andy.

Four years later, with only a handful of first team games to boast about, he left Parkhead as part of an exchange deal with goalkeeper Roy Baines, who is, ironically, back again at Cappielow.

And that was when Ritchie began to emerge as a truly great player. Now, at the age of twenty-three, he is Scotland's leading football entertainer.

Yet when he won the award he was a part-timer, devoting more time as Morton's pools agent to organizing the sale of the club's lottery tickets than he did to training.

Is he really idle, as so many say, a lad who doesn't like to lose sweat?

He grins: 'Well, I may not be the world's best trainer but I train as hard as anyone else at Cappielow. I must or manager Benny Rooney wouldn't pick me.

'I may not run as fast as other people but I do my share. I just don't accept that I'm a lazy player. I like to think I'm a skilful player and if I don't make tackles then we have players in the team to win the ball.'

Certainly no one entertains better than Andy Ritchie – Player of the Year, and rightly so.

THE NEW PELE SETS HAMPDEN ALIGHT

Saturday, 2 June, 1979, was yet another black day for Scottish football. A crowd of 61,918 turned out on an afternoon of bright sunshine to see Scotland face world champions Argentina at Hampden. And they realized there was a world of difference between the dazzling, fluent play of the men from South America and that of the Scots who faded once again after a fine start.

'Different class' – that was the sad summing up by everyone after Argentina had won 3-1.

But not one Scot would have missed this match. For we were given the privilege of seeing in action the young player who will be the new Pele, the new Cruyff, the new Di Stefano, the 18-year-old Argentinian wonder boy Diego Maradona. And that's one thing about the Scottish football supporter – he loves a truly gifted player. So how Maradona, built like a dreadnought, was cheered. For here, we realized, was one of the really greats. We were enjoying the treat of a lifetime, watching a lad who makes football a superb art, who is bursting out with talent.

Maradona was the architect of an easy victory for Argentina, now an even better side than that which won the World Cup by beating Holland in Buenos Aires.

He led his colleagues in turning Scotland outside in with magnificent ball control, menacing bursts, play that had the rippling rhythm of a symphony orchestra, the colour of a Disney fantasy, the polish of a Rolls Royce.

It was a chastening experience for Scotland. But Argentina were magic in the sun, showing off with elegant swerves, contemptuous flicks and impertinent control against a disjointed Scottish side who had little to offer except determination, guts and sweat.

But really it was Maradona who did the damage. For, as at Wembley against England, Scotland started well enough, playing with heart, pace and glimpses of that old-time artistry.

And then Maradona, a bouncing ball of a player, paralysed the men in blue with his bemusing runs, fantastic control and brilliant passes.

The kid who earns £100,000 a year (tax free) promised something special every time he touched the ball and Argentina exploited to the full Maradona's ability.

It was the new Pele who made the first goal, the goal that shattered Scotland. After Scotland had come close to scoring and the Argentinians had shown that they mixed glittering skills with a cynical ruthlessness that they cannot eradicate from their play, Maradona took over.

The shirt-sleeved fans watched incredulously as the little, squat lad turned on a lethal move that Pele couldn't have bettered. As if the ball was tied to his left foot, he waltzed round four Scottish defenders with incredible ease. The Scots were left

The new Pele, Argentina's wonder boy, Diego Maradona

Argentina in full flight at Hampden, and star striker Luque flashes past Paul Hegarty

bewildered. They just couldn't take the ball from the Argentinian magician, who suddenly flicked to World Cup star Luque. Alan Rough in the Scotland goal hadn't an earthly.

That was a goal worthy of winning a World Cup. And it took much of the heart out of Scotland.

When the second half started, the fans were cheering Argentina and unkindly booing their erstwhile heroes in blue.

And the Argentinians gave Scotland a lesson in scoring. Luque did the damage again when, with flawless finishing, he took on substitute goalkeeper George Wood on the left, leaving him floundering and sending the ball into the empty net from an acute angle.

That, however, was just the kind of quick, imaginative penetration which was the hallmark of the Argentinian play throughout a wonderful afternoon which contrasted so vividly with the ponderous play of the Scots.

It was the third goal that really set Hampden alight. It was scored with impertinence, with skill and a touch of humour by, naturally, Maradona. Frank Gray, replacing Asa Hartford in midfield, made a bad square pass. That proved fatal. Valencia pounced and pushed the ball on to Maradona.

So smartly, the magnificent senor controlled it, mesmerised Wood into leaving his line, feinted to cross, then to loft the ball under the bar and, with poor Wood as dazed as a rabbit gazing at a weasel, the little Argentinian as cool as you like cleverly planted the ball low between the keeper and the post.

What a goal! It was something out of a Glasgow Green match in cheek – but a goal only a star could have scored.

Near the end, Arthur Graham scored for Scotland, with the Argentinians protesting, claiming offside.

But that was poor consolation for Scotland, so outclassed. Only a fine display by new cap Iain Munro of St Mirren, at left back, brightened the gloom.

But then who could have beaten Argentina that sunny day?

They were entrancing and sent out a clear message that they are going to be the team to beat in the next World Cup in Spain.

And certainly Maradona is going to be an all-time great, long before he reaches his twenty-first birthday. Why, he is already.

Argentina gave Scotland a lesson in the science of football, the art of football, the poetry of football. And they also showed that you have to be hard to stay at the top. They chopped down Scottish attackers with monotonous regularity. And Scotland's patchwork side – in some cases manager Jock Stein had to make a third choice selection because of injuries – looked like football boys against the masters of the world.

There was no comparison between the teams. So Scotland realized – once again – just how much we have to learn, just how much we have to improve, just how much we have to strive for real teamwork, before we can have any chance of success at the top, before we can say we are among the elite of football.

As Argentinian manager Cesar Luis Menotti said: 'Scotland run too much to get the ball and once they get it are too tired to do much with it.'

The real lesson, however, was that Scotland, like so many other countries, lacks personality players.

Alas, there are few Maradonas around. Certainly not in Scotland.

The teams at Hampden were:

Scotland: Rough (Partick Thistle), Burley (Ipswich Town), Hegarty (Dundee United), Hansen (Liverpool), Munro (St

Mirren), Narey (Dundee United), Wark (Ipswich Town), Hartford (Manchester City), McGarvey (Liverpool), Dalglish (Liverpool), Graham (Leeds United)
Subs: Wood (Everton), Gray (Leeds United), Wallace (Coventry City), Jordan (Manchester United), Miller (Aberdeen)
Argentina: Fillol, Olguin, Villaverde, Passarella, Tarantini, Barbas, Gallego, Maradona, Houseman, Luque, Valencia
Subs: Trossero, Outes, Baley, Oviedo, Reinaldi, Perotti
Referee: P. Partridge, England

All the Argentina thrills. Trossero vaults over Frank McGarvey of Scotland at Hampden

CELTIC'S NIGHT OF NIGHTS – Super end to the greatest League race

It was the most dramatic night Scottish football has ever known, the night of the greatest Old Firm battle of them all, the night when Celtic and Rangers had a 52,000 crowd at Parkhead on their toes as they fought for Scottish soccer's most valuable and coveted prize – the Premier League title.

It was the night of Monday, 21 May 1979, the climax of a remarkable season. Severe weather had made a shambles of Scottish football and, because of postponements, the season went on and on. Nevertheless, it was the keenest Premier League championship race, with fortunes fluctuating, clubs challenging and falling away and a nail-biting finish assured. And what a finish!

What it boiled down to was that if Celtic won the last match of the season against their oldest rivals, Rangers, at Parkhead they would take the title. If they lost, the championship would almost certainly be retained by Rangers, who had games in hand.

The game will be talked about, relived for all time for it was the most legendary Old Firm match of all.

The record reveals that Celtic clinched the championship by beating Rangers 4–2 on a pleasant spring evening but statistics alone will never be able to tell the tale of 90 minutes of football, passion and courage the likes of which none of the crowd, so hoarse at the end, had ever seen.

Said Celtic manager Billy McNeill after-wards: 'If this match had been written for a boys magazine no one would have believed it.' No one indeed.

For Celtic came off the ropes not once, not twice, but three times to clinch a victory as memorable as anything achieved by the Lisbon Lions or any of the magnificent Parkhead teams of the past. The endless courage, dynamic determination and resolute reserves of stamina which carried Celtic from virtually nowhere to the title were displayed in glorious technicolor. No words can convey the colour, the drama, the triumph and tragedy of the match.

But it was probably the best match, in terms of excitement, of the century.

Celtic driving on from the start were caught in nine minutes by a clever goal. Rangers winger Davie Cooper ran sweetly down the wing, beat two defenders and sent over a perfect cross for Alex MacDonald to knock the ball past Peter Latchford.

And by half time Celtic, although pressing incessantly, were still behind to that choice goal. Rangers were playing it skilfully, in the Continental manner, putting the accent on defence, and Celtic, despite all their heroics, all their heart-stopping assaults, couldn't find a way through.

It looked all over for them when soon after the second half had begun winger Johnny Doyle foolishly aimed a kick at the prone figure of Alex MacDonald, who had been fouled, and was sent off.

Few now gave Celtic any chance. Their luck was out for when Roy Aitken had

'We've done it' – and triumphant Celtic celebrate after winning the Premier League

'We've lost it' – the picture that expresses all the Rangers woe at losing the Premier League title. Goalkeeper Peter McCloy sits disconsolately after his team's defeat at Parkhead

earlier hit the junction of bar and post with a magnificent header which had Peter McCloy beaten all the way, it seemed the fates had conspired to mock them.

But that ordering off proved to be the turning point of the match. It steeled Celtic to even greater efforts, forced them to tap sources of energy they didn't know existed, made them all the more determined not to accept defeat.

And suddenly it all came right for the bravest of all Celtic teams – and went sour for a Rangers side who appeared bewildered by the do-or-die efforts of their rivals.

The equaliser came in 67 minutes – to a tremendous cheer.

A cute flick from Davie Provan was turned into the net by Roy Aitken whose display will forever be imprinted on the minds of those who saw this young, stalwart Celt become a crusader, a new Duncan Edwards.

And then the unbelievable – Celtic took the lead. An Aitken drive was blocked, the ball broke to George McCluskey whose superb shot beat McCloy and put the home fans in a seventh heaven.

But suddenly the supporters in green and white were brought back to earth with a cruel thump – the fascinating script still had plenty of twists to offer.

Rangers at last hit back and when a Cooper corner broke to Robert Russell, the stylish Ranger smashed a low drive through a posse of players and into the net. And Rangers were again looking good for the point that would satisfy them.

'That,' said Billy McNeill later, 'was when our team had to climb another mountain. They thought they had done it when George McCluskey put us in front. But they had reached the top only to find another hill looming. But they did it and I couldn't be prouder of them.'

Again Celtic wound themselves up. Again they came back. Roy Aitken must have been near to tears when another fine header was miraculously saved by Peter McCloy.

Who could stop this proud Celtic side now? Not Rangers.

And the fairytale for Parkhead came true when poor Colin Jackson, who had enjoyed such a splendid season for Rangers, involuntarily headed the ball into his own net after a McCluskey cross was pushed out by McCloy.

There was no way back this time for Rangers – and Murdo MacLeod emphasized Celtic's superiority when he slammed a wonderful shot into the Rangers net almost on time, a superb goal.

And that was one for the *Guinness Book of Records*. For Celtic had scored four goals against Rangers with only ten men on the field.

So Celtic were the Scottish champions – really great champions. They proved that with a display of fantastic football unsurpassed by any of the heroes of the Parkhead past – a torrid, heart-stopping, courageous display that had everything that is superb in Scottish football.

And so the head-shaking by even the most fervent Celtic supporters who had insisted all season that their team just wasn't good enough stopped. For they realized that any side who played the way those young Celts did in one of the most dramatic games Scottish football has known, must be great.

It wasn't soccer in the silken, languid style. It wasn't soccer that bore the hallmark of elegance, of grace. It wasn't the soccer the purists dream about.

But it was the most exciting soccer we have seen in a decade – the football Scots really like best. It was fiercely competitive, roaringly exploited on the wings and down the centre, powerful, compelling, physical and tough but laced with skill shown at top pace . . . wonderful.

It was a fitting end to a hard-fought Premier League which promises to be even more exciting this season, with the Old Firm again battling and, hopefully, challenges from teams like Hibernian, Aberdeen and Dundee United even keener.

The teams on that incredible Parkhead night were:

Celtic are in seventh heaven as Murdo MacLeod makes it 4–2 at Parkhead

Celtic: Latchford, McGrain, Lynch, Aitken, McAdam, Edvaldsson, Provan, Conroy, McCluskey, MacLeod, Doyle
Subs: Davidson, Lennox
Rangers: McCloy, Jardine, Dawson, Johnstone, Jackson, MacDonald, McLean, Russell, Parlane, Smith, Cooper
Subs: Miller, Watson
Referee: E. Pringle, Edinburgh